B-29 SUPERFORTRESS
VS
JAPANESE NIGHTFIGHTER

Japan 1944–45

MARK LARDAS

OSPREY

Bloomsbury Publishing Plc
Kemp House, Chawley Park, Cumnor Hill, Oxford, OX2 9PH, UK
29 Earlsfort Terrace, Dublin 2, Ireland
1385 Broadway, 5th Floor, New York, NY 10018, USA
E-mail: info@ospreypublishing.com

OSPREY is a trademark of Osprey Publishing Ltd

First published in Great Britain in 2025

A catalogue record for this book is available from the British Library.

ISBN: PB: 9781472865601; eBook 9781472865618; ePDF 9781472865588;
XML 9781472865595

25 26 27 28 29 10 9 8 7 6 5 4 3 2 1

Edited by Tony Holmes
Cover artwork and battlescene by Gareth Hector
Three-views, cockpit views and armament views by Jim Laurier
Map and tactical diagram by www.bounford.com
Index by Mark Swift
Typeset by PDQ Digital Media Solutions, Bungay, UK
Printed by Repro India Ltd

Osprey Publishing supports the Woodland Trust, the UK's leading woodland
conservation charity.

To find out more about our authors and books visit
www.ospreypublishing.com. Here you will find extracts, author interviews,
details of forthcoming events and the option to sign up for our newsletter.

Author's Dedication
I would like to dedicate this volume to my friends at the Gulf-Bay Area
Modelers Association, specifically Fitz Walker III, for their interest in and
support of my writing.

Acknowledgements
The author would like to thank Fitz Walker III and Nanci Omori for
translating Japanese text describing the Ki-45 cockpit components. Without
their help I could not have completed the annotation for the artwork. All
mistakes remain my own, though.

J1N1-S "Irving" cover artwork
This J1N1-S pilot spent five minutes stalking his target on the night of 25–26
May, 1945. It was a long, slow chase, closing cautiously to avoid alerting his
prey as the nightfighter flew over fires consuming Tokyo thousands of feet
below the aircraft. Just before he reached the perfect firing position, B-29
42-65281 *MISS AMERICA '62* of the 24th BS/8th BG, which had been flying
straight and level (ideal for an attack) over the Japanese capital, abruptly
turned and sped up. Knowing his nightfighter could not keep up with an
alerted bomber, the IJNAF pilot took his shot. A burst of 20mm rounds arced
skyward, only to miss the fuselage. A few shells struck the left wingtip. Was it
enough to bring down the bomber? The J1N1-S pilot hoped so, but suspected
his quarry would make it home. (Artwork by Gareth Hector)

B-29 Superfortress cover artwork
The B-29 left side gunner sat at his station knew that on this night raid (the
very last nocturnal fire-bombing mission to target Tokyo) he was only an
observer, for the turret guns he controlled were unloaded. The only bullets
carried were in the rear turret – the bomber's solitary manned position. But
even as an observer, he knew he played a critical role in the aircraft's safety. If
he spotted a nightfighter before it attacked he could alert the crew, allowing
the pilots to take evasive action – a B-29 could outrun any Japanese twin-
engined nightfighter if given adequate warning of an attack. He kept especially
alert during the 15 minutes over the target. That was the mission's danger
point. Suddenly, he saw something behind and below his aircraft (B-29
42-65281 *MISS AMERICA '62* of the 24th BS/8th BG). He shouted a
warning, and the B-29 swerved and accelerated. He watched a short stream of
cannon fire arcing up to the bomber's left, and shudders seconds later meant
something had hit the wingtip. The damage looked minor, however. (Artwork
by Gareth Hector)

Previous Page
Pilots and observers from 302nd Kokutai pose for an official photograph in
front of a J1N1-S at Atsugi on January 1, 1945. Gekko ace Lt Sachio Endo is
sat in the second row, seventh from left, directly beneath the nose of the
nightfighter. (Tony Holmes Collection)

CONTENTS

Introduction   4

Chronology   7

Design and Development   9

Technical Specifications   21

The Strategic Situation   35

The Combatants   40

Combat   50

Statistics and Analysis   73

Aftermath   77

Further Reading   79

Index   80

INTRODUCTION

The Japanese knew an air raid was coming. They had had their first warning even before it started. Signal intelligence detected the pre-mission checks the B-29s' radio operators performed with their equipment prior to takeoff. These told them it would be a big raid, perhaps the biggest yet. Hundreds of radio checks were counted. An alert went out to the chain of picket boats and the Imperial Japanese Army (IJA) and Imperial Japanese Navy (IJN) radar stations guarding the approaches to Japan.

The IJN initially detected the enemy bombers through its early-warning picket boats. By March 1945 there were fewer of these, but there were still enough to spot aircraft flying overhead. The next warning came from an IJN radar station on Hachijo-Jima, 178 miles southeast of Tokyo in the Philippine Sea. This small volcanic island was part of a chain administrated by the Japanese, being the outermost one of three that featured radar stations. It was on the path B-29s had to follow to reach Honshu, Japan's largest Home Island and its industrial heart.

IJN early-warning radar had a range of 155 miles, so the enemy aircraft were detected nearly 300 miles from the Japanese coast. That gave at least an hour's warning

The Japanese knew when a raid was imminent even before the first bomber had taken off from runways in the Marianas. Signal intelligence gave the IJNAF and IJAAF at least five hours warning before the bombers' arrival over their target. Taxiing out to start a mission from North Field, on Tinian, this particular aircraft, 42-24759 *AMIABLE AMAZON* of the 6th BG/313th BW, was one of three B-29s lost by the group during the largest attack ever launched against Tokyo on May 23–24, 1945. (National Museum of the Air Force (NMAF))

of the approaching B-29s. More realistically it was closer to 90 minutes, since the bombers were at their fuel-efficient overwater cruise speed of 235mph and most targets, including Tokyo, were not on the coast, but on the inland side of deep harbors. Imperial Japanese Naval Air Force (IJNAF) fighter units would be scrambled to intercept and IJN bases placed on alert.

Perhaps the IJN passed the warning of a raid on to its IJA rivals, or possibly not, for the IJN and IJA avoided communicating with each other. The IJN disliked the IJA almost as much as it hated the enemy. Distain was mutual. The IJA radar stations on the coast of Japan provided it with independent confirmation of the approaching enemy 124 miles from Japan's coast, giving 30 minutes' warning. This was enough time to scramble Imperial Japanese Army Air Force (IJAAF) units and get them to the expected altitude (30,000ft) at which the bombers were approaching. If the defending fighters were launched earlier than 30 minutes prior to the attack, they would waste fuel waiting for the enemy to arrive. Fuel was both scarce and precious.

By the time fighters were launching on the evening of March 9, 1945, it was obvious the target was the Greater Tokyo Area. A sprawling mix of three cities, it included Japan's largest and fifth largest cities (Tokyo and Yokohama, respectively) linked by the smaller (ninth largest) but sizable Kawasaki. Ten million people lived there. It was Japan's greatest industrial complex. The US Army Air Force (USAAF) had been bombing the Greater Tokyo Area since November 1944 without doing much damage. The worst raid, two weeks earlier on February 25, had resulted in a square mile of Tokyo being burned out.

This new raid was different. The first US bombers had left their bases in the Marianas at 1815 hrs Tokyo time. They began arriving over the city at 0100 hrs on March 10. Prior to this mission, most B-29 raids had been daylight attacks. Although a few ineffective night missions had been made in 1944 by China-based B-29s, US Army Air Force (USAAF) units flying from the Marianas had hitherto avoided nocturnal operations. One disadvantage of a night raid for the Japanese was they could only sortie nightfighters. By 1945, few pilots were night qualified, and the IJNAF and IJAAF generally had only one group of twin-engined nightfighters in each air division, including those guarding Tokyo. The other difference was this raid was bigger than most.

Regardless, by the time the B-29s began arriving, the Japanese nightfighters were circling at 28,000–30,000ft – the altitude at which US bombers had always previously flown over the Home Islands. IJAAF and IJNAF crews had to use past performance for their guide, as Japanese radar only gave range and bearing, not aircraft altitude. Once aloft, pilots were on their own. They got no further information from the ground. The circling hunters found nothing.

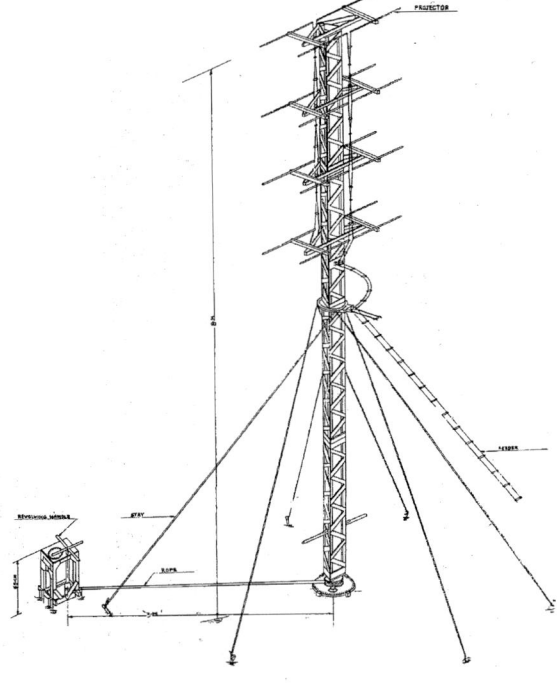

The antenna array for the IJN's Type 3, Mark 1, Model 3 early-warning radar. Serving as a long-range search and detection system, it had a range of 155 miles. Type 3, Mark 1, Model 3 radar guarded the eastern approaches to Tokyo. (Author's Collection)

The aftermath of the March 9–10, 1945 fire raid on Tokyo was widespread devastation. The attack, centered on the Asakusa ward, burned out 15.8 square miles of the city. Asakusa was the most densely built-up area of Tokyo at the time. This photograph shows damage typical of an attack with incendiaries. (Author's Collection)

There were no enemy aircraft at 30,000ft. They were miles lower, coming in between 4,900–9,200ft.

The nightfighter pilots' first indication they had been caught out of position to intercept their foe was when Tokyo began erupting in flames below them as incendiaries started to land. Their searches became more frantic. Tokyo was burning below them, but they were finding no enemy bombers. They were slow to realize what had happened. The IJAAF nightfighters lacked radar, and the scopes in the few IJNAF aircraft carrying such equipment were blank as their maximum detection range was just 1.86 miles. The US bombers some 3.7 miles (and 20,000ft) below them were out of range. By the time they did react it was too late. Tokyo was ablaze and a fire storm was starting. During the course of the mission B-29 crews reported only 76 nightfighter sightings and just 40 attacks. All were unsuccessful.

The results achieved by the raid exceeded the most optimistic expectations of Maj Gen Curtis LeMay, commander of the Twentieth Air Force's XXI Bomber Command. Nearly 16 square miles of Tokyo, centered in the Asakusa district (its most densely-built quarter), was incinerated. Gone was one-fifth of the Asakusa's industrial area and two-thirds of its commercial area. The death toll was high, with estimates ranging from 83,000 to 135,000. LeMay had found the key to making the B-29 a war-winning tool – the night fire raid.

Only one thing could stop the onslaught – nightfighters. Japan did not have enough antiaircraft guns to repel a fire raid, except, possibly, by concentrating all of its weapons in one city and leaving the rest of the country undefended. But antiaircraft artillery proved vulnerable to fire raids, with gun batteries being burned out as the conflagration spread. The IJAAF and IJNAF had few nightfighters, but they were mobile and could be concentrated where needed.

The first Tokyo fire raid marked the start of a four-month struggle between B-29s and Japan's nightfighter force. It was a true duel between two aircraft, a single B-29 against a single nightfighter, in the ultimate game of hide-and-seek. Whoever spotted their opponent first would succeed, with the onus very much being on the nightfighter to find the bomber. The stakes were high. If nightfighters shot down a sufficient number of B-29s, the nocturnal bomber campaign was doomed. If they did not, Japan was.

CHRONOLOGY

1937
March   IJAAF orders development of a twin-engined two-seat fighter.

December   IJAAF instructs Kawasaki to commence work on the Ki-45.

1938
June   The IJNAF issues Mitsubishi and Nakajima with a request calling for a land-based, long-range twin-engined escort fighter. Nakajima agrees to design one.

1939
January   Following the establishment of a requirement by the US Army Air Corps (USAAC) for a "super bomber," Boeing commences work on designing its Model 333 four-engined aircraft, which would lead to the creation of the B-29 Superfortress.

January   First flight of the Ki-45 prototype.

March   The IJNAF issues design specifications for what becomes the Nakajima J1N1 fighter.

December 2   US Department of War issues a Request For Proposals (RFP) for a very long-range heavy "super bomber."

1940
February 5   The USAAC issues a specification for a "super bomber," with the aircraft being significantly larger than the existing B-17 and B-24 four-engined bombers then flying.

May 11   Boeing submits its Model 335 design to the USAAC as a "super bomber" RFP response.

September 6   The USAAC signs contracts with Boeing to produce the B-29 Superfortress.

1941
May 2   J1N1 prototype makes its first flight.

September   Ki-45 KAI, with improved performance thanks to more powerful engines and airframe redesign, flies for the first time. IJAAF accepts it for production.

October   IJNAF rejects the J1N1 as a fighter, but approves its production as a reconnaissance aircraft.

December 7   IJNAF carrier-based aircraft attack Pearl Harbor, bringing the US into World War II.

1942
July   Rabaul-based Tainan Kokutai (air group) commences operational trials with three J1N1-Cs (given the Allied reporting name "Irving") in the reconnaissance role.

August   Ki-45 (given the Allied reporting name "Nick") enters service as a day long-range escort fighter.

September 21   First flight of the prototype B-29.

November 20   Cdr Yasuna Kozono, commanding officer of 251st Kokutai, proposes arming J1N1-Cs with obliquely-firing 20mm cannon for nightfighting operations. The IJNAF planning staff reject his proposal.

1943
April   251st Kokutai is sent to Vunakanau airfield in Rabaul, on the island of New Britain, equipped with 58 A6M3 Zero-sen and two J1N1-Cs.

May   A third J1N1-C recently delivered to 251st Kokutai is modified into a nightfighter by fitting Type 99 20mm cannon firing obliquely

	upward and downward at 30 degrees azimuth.
May 21	PO1c Shigetoshi Kudo shoots down two B-17E Flying Fortress bombers at night with the modified J1N1-C. He subsequently downs four more B-17s and a B-24D Liberator at night over the next two months.
July	IJAAF units in New Guinea field-modify Ki-45 KAIas with obliquely firing 12.7mm machine guns for use as nightfighters.
August	Production of the J1N1-S nightfighter begins.
September	Kawasaki commences production of the Ki-45 KAIc nightfighter.

1944

March	IJAAF and IJNAF reorganize home air defense against expected B-29 attacks.
June 15–16	Imperial Iron and Steel Works at Yawata, in Fukuoka Prefecture, bombed in the first B-29 mission against Japan.
June 15	Saipan invaded by US forces.
June	IJNAF successfully defeats an attempt to create a joint IJAAF–IJNAF air defense force for the Japanese Home Islands.
July 21	Guam invaded by US forces.
July 24	Saipan invaded by US forces.
October 12	B-29s arrive at Isley Field on Saipan.
November 10	Harmon Field on Guam is declared operational and open to B-29s.
November 24	First B-29 mission against Japan launched from the Marianas. Tokyo bombed by 111 B-29s from Saipan.
December 27	North Field in Tinian becomes operational with the arrival of B-29s.
December	Production ceases for the Ki-45 and J1N1.

1945

January 21	Maj Gen Curtis LeMay takes charge of XXI Bomber Command.
February 4	Experimental incendiary raid on Kobe. It fails due to the small

	number of bombers involved and the high-altitude release of ordnance.
February 19	US Marine Corps invades Iwo Jima.
March 4	First B-29 makes an emergency landing on Iwo Jima.
March 9–10	First mass incendiary raid on Tokyo. More than 267,000 buildings are burned out and in excess of 83,000 killed.
March 9–18	Five major incendiary raids launched in a ten-day period. Tokyo, Nagoya, Kobe and Osaka attacked.
March 16	Central Field on Iwo Jima becomes operational.
March 27	313th Bombardment Wing (BW) begins mining operations in the Straits of Shimonoseki to open Operation *Starvation*.
April 1	Okinawa invaded by US forces.
April 6	Kadena airfield on Okinawa opens as an emergency landing site for B-29s.
April 7	Superfortress barrage and spot jamming of Japanese fire control radars employed for the first time.
April 13–16	Incendiary attacks target the Greater Tokyo Area.
May 14	Between May 14 and June 10, six of Japan's ten largest cities are burned out in multi-bomb wing maximum effort raids.
June 17	Incendiary attacks on Japan's secondary cities begin. They continue until war's end.
August 6	B-29 44-86292 *ENOLA GAY* of the 393rd Bombardment Squadron (BS)/509th Composite Group (CG) drops an atomic bomb on Hiroshima.
August 8	The Soviet Union declares war on Japan.
August 9	B-29 44-27297 *BOCKSCAR* of the 393rd BS/509th CG drops an atomic bomb on Nagasaki.
August 15	Japan surrenders.
August 16	B-29 production ceases with 3,970 examples completed. Aircraft on assembly lines are scrapped in place.

DESIGN AND DEVELOPMENT

BOEING B-29 SUPERFORTRESS

The B-29 was World War II's ultimate expression of the strategic bomber, a long-range aircraft capable of carrying a large bombload. Air power theory held that strategic bombers could eliminate an enemy's ability to wage war by destroying its logistical and command infrastructure. By bombing its factories, administrative centers and transportation network, strategic bombers would render an enemy incapable of continuing to fight.

Strategic bombing had its origins in World War I, when Germany using Zeppelins and long-range multi-engined bombers to attack targets in England. After the US entered the war, Brig Gen Billy Mitchell advocated using massed bombers to circumvent the trench stalemate. Britain built strategic bombers in World War I, with twin-engined (O/100) and four-engined (O/400) Handley-Page aircraft entering service. The New Jersey-based Standard Aircraft Corporation duly built sets of components for the O-400 (US designation) in 1918, which were then shipped to Britain for assembly – more than 100 had been delivered by war's end. In 1919, eight O-400s were assembled locally for the US Army, and they were flown into the early 1920s. However, World War I era aircraft soon proved to be too fragile for sustained post-war operations, so the US abandoned the big bomber during the 1920s.

Advances in aeronautical engineering caused the USAAC and the Royal Air Force (RAF) to rethink the heavy bomber. By the early 1930s, all-metal aircraft were

The one-off Boeing XB-15 was the first all-metal, four-engined monoplane bomber in the USAAC's inventory. Underpowered, it served as a proof-of-concept test bed. The aircraft (seen here with another Boeing product in the form of a P-26 "Peashooter" acting as a chase plane) ended its career as the XC-105 transport, before being retired in December 1944. (Author's Collection)

appearing, and they were significantly stronger than the canvas-and-wood types fielded in World War I and the 1920s. Monoplanes, inherently faster than biplanes, became practical. Features like retractable landing gear and internal bomb-bays were easier to incorporate, and much larger aircraft were possible, given metal's greater inherent strength.

Fighters, tactical bombers and observation aircraft had always formed part of the USAAC doctrine. Yet it still believed in the potential of strategic bombers. The US had a larger industrial base than Britain, which meant it was more able to experiment with the development of large bombers. All-metal aircraft and the increasingly powerful aero engines being developed throughout the 1930s gave the US opportunities to design bigger and better prototypes that had the potential to be true strategic bombers.

In 1935 the USAAC ordered Boeing to construct the XB-15 – the largest bomber built up to then. While it never went into production, the aircraft was the precursor of American four-engined bombers of World War II. All metal, it could carry 12,000lb of bombs and had a combat range of 3,400 miles. Underpowered due to the engines then available, only one XB-15 was built. Nevertheless, the experience Boeing gained building the aircraft allowed it to design a downsized version, the four-engined Model 299. The company offered the prototype, built at its expense, to the USAAC in response to the latter's RFP for a multi-engined bomber.

The Model 299 was clearly superior to the two twin-engined entries in the bomber competition organized by the USAAC. It was faster, carried more ordnance and had a greater range. However, a certain victory was lost when the Model 299 crashed due to pilot error. The contract went to the Douglas design, which became the B-18 Bolo. Yet the USAAC had been sufficiently impressed by the Boeing bomber that in 1936 it ordered 13 Model 299s for "experimental" purposes as the YB-17. These in turn led to the B-17 Flying Fortress, which entered service as the USAAC's first heavy bomber in 1939. It also led to development of the B-24 Liberator by Consolidated. Both aircraft served as the backbone of the USAAF's heavy bomber force in World War II.

The B-17 and B-24 whetted the USAAC's desire for a bigger bomber. Called "Project A," it sought an intercontinental bomber capable of traveling 5,000 miles. The program led Boeing to develop the Model 316 in 1937 and Models 333 and 334 two years later. The Model 316 was an update of the XB-15, with more powerful engines. It got as far as an order for two prototypes (designated the Y1B-20), but they were cancelled before work began on them. The Model 344 never progressed beyond the mock-up stage. Developed in 1938–39, it could carry 2,000lb of bombs 5,000 miles at up to 350mph. The aircraft would have also had a pressurized cabin and a shoulder-mounted high-aspect wing.

During the same period Douglas developed the design for what became the XB-19. Another four-engined aircraft, it was the biggest American bomber built until the Convair B-36 "Peacemaker" appeared in 1946. As with the XB-15, the XB-19 was a one-off. Indeed, it took so long to build the prototype that the aircraft was obsolete before it first flew in June 1941.

On February 5, 1940 the USAAC issued a specification for a "super bomber," one significantly larger than the existing B-17 and B-24 four-engined bombers then flying. This new aircraft was to be capable of carrying 20,000lb of bombs to a target 2,700 miles distant. It was to operate at high altitudes, 30,000ft and above. By contrast, the B-24, which had made its maiden flight on December 29, 1939, was capable of carrying only 2,700lb of bombs 1,200 miles. It was an ambitious request.

Four manufacturers responded with designs – Boeing, Lockheed, Douglas and Consolidated. Boeing delivered its proposal on May 11, 1940 in the form of the Model 335. It was designated XB-29. Lockheed's design was the L-249, which the USAAC designated the XB-30. Douglas offered the Model 332, designated the XB-31, and, finally, Consolidated's four-engined Model 33 became the XB-32. A preliminary examination by USAAC evaluators revealed Boeing's entry as clearly superior to the other three. The latter trio were upsized versions of each manufacturer's existing four-engined designs. Lockheed's L-249 used the L-049 Constellation transport as its basis, Douglas had revamped its existing XB-19 and the Consolidated Model 34 was derived from the then new B-24. Boeing used the Model 334 as its starting point.

The Model 335 possessed a pressurized cabin. While the cabin was depressurized during combat, it allowed the crew to work in a shirtsleeve environment during the cruise phase, reducing fatigue at high altitudes. Neither the XB-30 nor XB-31 offered a pressurized cabin. The B-32 did, but Consolidated had never built a pressurized design before submitting the XB-32. Boeing had – the company's Model 307 Stratoliner airliner, which had first flown in 1938 and entered airline service in 1940, was pressurized.

Boeing dubbed the Model 335 the Superfortress, linking it to the B-17. It was well named, being superlative in virtually every way. The aircraft had a ceiling of 32,000ft, a top speed of 357mph and it could cruise at 220mph. Manned by a crew of 11, the Model 335 could carry 5,000lb of bombs 1,600 miles at 30,000ft.

The aircraft was armed with 12 0.50-cal. machine guns and one 20mm cannon. Boeing initially resisted arming the B-29, its design being aerodynamically perfect,

The USAAC ordered the B-32 Dominator from Consolidated, even though it believed the bomber was inferior to the B-29 – the aircraft was viewed as insurance against the Superfortress's failure. The B-29 flew and saw combat before to the less-advanced B-32. (NMAF)

99ft 0in.

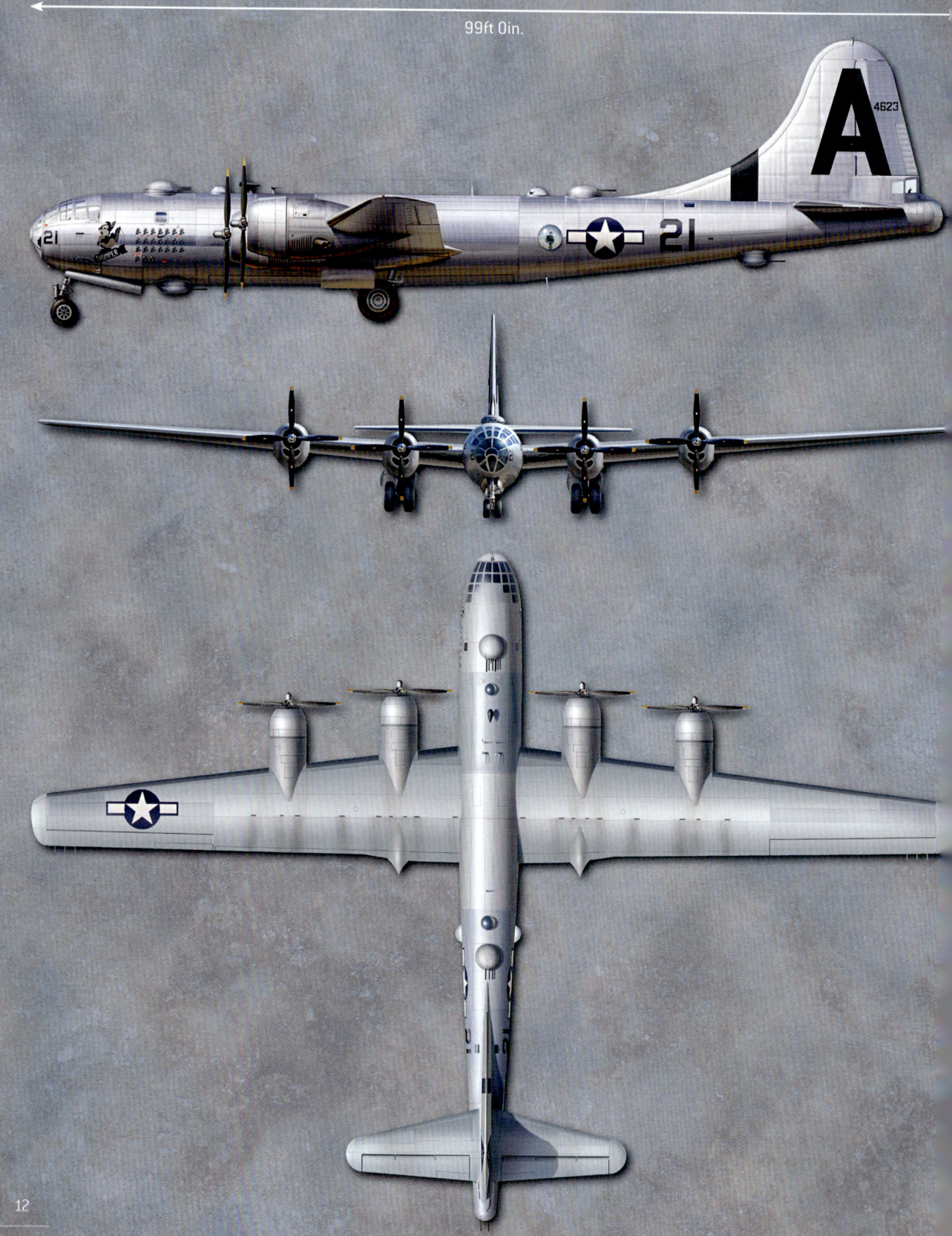

141ft 3in.

with no external scoops or vents interrupting its lines. The rivets were flush with the skin to reduce drag. Adding manned turrets would destroy the aerodynamics and make a pressurized cabin impossible. As a compromise, Boeing opted to use remotely controlled, unmanned turrets that used a system developed by General Electric to aim the guns. This Central Fire Control System allowed all turrets to be operated by any of the gunners aboard the aircraft.

The Superfortress was so clearly superior to its rivals that the USAAC cancelled the XB-30 and XB-31. The B-32 program was kept alive as an alternative should the revolutionary B-29 fail. On August 29, 1940, the USAAC ordered two XB-29 prototypes from Boeing. By April 1941 the company had completed a full-scale mockup of the aircraft. By then, a scale model had successfully completed wind tunnel tests. Due to looming wartime pressure, the USAAC lacked time to build a prototype, leisurely work out its bugs and then put the aircraft into production. Instead, on May 17, 1941, the USAAC placed orders for 14 test YB-29s and 250 production B-29s. It was not until September 21, 1942, however, that the first XB-29 took to the air.

By then, the USAAF had issued Boeing with orders exceeding 250 examples, resulting in production lines being set up in four different locations – Renton, Washington, Wichita, Kansas, Marietta, Georgia, and Bellevue, Nebraska. Boeing operated the Renton and Wichita plants, while Bell and Martin ran the Marietta and Bellevue facilities, respectively. The USAAF would eventually commit $3 billion to the building of B-29s by war's end, making it the costliest program of the war.

Development of the Superfortress was troubled. The aircraft's quartet of Wright R-3350 Duplex-Cyclone radial engines initially proved unreliable, frequently catching fire. The second XB-29 had an engine fire on its first flight, and a subsequent conflagration in February 1943 resulted in the aircraft's destruction and the death of all on board. Because the B-29 went into production before being fully tested, constant post-production field modifications were required on early examples. Delays in these

OPPOSITE

B-29-40-BW 42-24623 *THUMPER* rolled off the Boeing Wichita production line in July 1944, the bomber subsequently being delivered to the 870th BS/497th BG on the very last day of that same month. Flying from Isley Field, Saipan, *THUMPER* was the first Superfortress to complete 40 combat missions, after which it was then sent back to the United States to undertake a War Bond tour. This artwork shows how the bomber appeared on July 7, 1945, when it participated in an incendiary raid on Akashi. *THUMPER*'s gunners were credited with no fewer than 20 aerial victories, six of them being claimed on the January 27, 1945 mission to Tokyo. The veteran bomber was sold as scrap in November 1950 following several years held in reserve with thousands of other aircraft at Pyote AFB, Texas.

changes meant few B-29s were airworthy during the first months of 1944. To send the Superfortress into combat from airfields in India and China in spring 1944 required a major maintenance push – dubbed the "Battle of Wichita" – during March of that year.

By the summer of 1944 sufficient problems had been solved to permit production of reliable aircraft, with nearly 500 B-29s having been manufactured by July. From September, monthly production exceeded 120, and this had increased to 300 per month by March 1945. It never fell below 300 per month before war's end. While B-29s continued to have engine issues, the bomber had become a war-winning aircraft by January 1945 – if effective means to use it could be found.

JAPANESE NIGHTFIGHTERS

When World War II commenced in September 1939, no air arms were equipped with dedicated nightfighters. Pre-war bomber doctrine favored daylight attacks so that crews could see their targets. When the number of bombers lost during daylight raids proved too high, nations switched to nocturnal missions.

Initially, to counter these night raids, conventional single-engined pursuit fighters were used to intercept bombers. They generally proved ineffective. Early nocturnal bomber missions saw aircraft flying individually in streams. For fighter pilots sent up to intercept such raiders, simply finding a target in the reduced visibility of night took time – often more time than the limited fuel of a single-engined fighter permitted. Unaided night navigation also proved daunting in the crowded cockpit of a single-seat interceptor.

Most nations soon turned to twin-engined aircraft to undertake the nightfighter role. While dedicated designs like the Luftwaffe's He 219 and the USAAF's P-61 Black Widow eventually emerged, the first truly effective nightfighters were conversions of twin-engined heavy fighters and light bombers capable of being fitted with radar. The RAF and USAAF initially converted light bombers (the Blenheim I and P-70 Havoc, respectively), before the British progressed to the superlative Beaufighter and Mosquito. The Luftwaffe also modified twin-engined bombers into nightfighters (most notably the Do 217 and Ju 88), although it more commonly relied on the twin-engined Bf 110 *Zerstörer* heavy fighter.

Pioneered by Germany, the heavy fighter emerged in the mid-1930s. Believed to hold several advantages over single-engined interceptors, the heavy fighter could be fitted with increased armament. The first generation of monoplane single-engined fighters typically carried two rifle-caliber or 0.50-cal. machine guns. Early versions of the Bf 110, however, were fitted with two fixed 20mm cannon and four 7.92mm machine guns grouped in the nose, plus a single flexibly mounted 7.92mm weapon for the rear gunner. The *Zerstörer* was as fast as contemporary single-engined fighters, and had a longer range. It could also fly with one engine out, thus improving survivability. The aircraft was, however, appreciably less maneuverable than a single-engined fighter.

The Bf 110 had a two-man crew, with the rear gunner being able to relieve the pilot of navigation duties. The protection offered by the gunner was believed adequate compensation for the lack of maneuverability. Pre-war at least, the Bf 110 was seemingly a multi-mission aircraft that could do it all. Fitted with bomb racks, it could serve as a tactical fighter-bomber, and the installation of cameras allowed the aircraft to undertake the reconnaissance role. Nations widely imitated the Bf 110 after its appearance in prototype form in 1936.

Japan enthusiastically embraced the heavy fighter concept, with the IJAAF issuing an official specification for such a type as early as March 1937 when it sent requests for proposals to Nakajima, Mitsubishi and Kawasaki. It chose the Kawasaki design for further development, designating it Ki-38. A twin-engined, single-seat design, with inline liquid-cooled engines, it saw wind-tunnel testing and completion of a full-scale mockup. The IJAAF suspended further work on the Ki-38 in October 1937, deciding the original requirements were inadequate.

The Ki-45 began its career as the IJAAF's heavy fighter. While it had excellent range and powerful armament, the aircraft lacked maneuverability to the point where it needed an escort when opposed by modern single-engined fighters. The Toryu's stability and firepower made it an obvious choice to serve as a nightfighter. (Tony Holmes Collection)

It reissued a specification to Kawasaki in December, calling for a two-crew aircraft capable of reaching 335mph that could operate at altitudes between 6,500–16,500ft and with a range of 1,025 miles, allowing 30 minutes of combat. The specification required two forward-firing cannon and a flexible rear-firing machine gun. Kawasaki's response was the Ki-45, a modified Ki-38 that had had its inline engines replaced with radial air-cooled powerplants. It was armed with a forward-firing 20mm Ho-3 cannon in a ventral tunnel on the starboard underside of the fuselage, two fixed 7.7mm Type 89 machine guns in the upper fuselage nose and a flexible rear-firing 7.7mm Type 89 machine gun. Development progressed slowly, with the prototype finally flying for the first time in January 1939. Flight trials proved disappointing, with the prototype being underpowered, stall prone, and with engines (Nakajima Ha-20bs) that failed with consistent regularity.

The IJAAF was determined to have a heavy fighter, however. Kawasaki refined the design over the next 20 months, twice replacing the engines with more powerful and reliable powerplants before the aircraft was finally accepted when fitted with Nakajima Ha-25s. The Ki-45 became operational in August 1942 as a long-range bomber escort, the IJAAF calling it Toryu (Dragonslayer).

The IJNAF independently developed its own heavy fighter after the IJAAF had contracted Kawasaki to build the Ki-45, and the aircraft was never intended for carrier-based operations. The IJNAF could, therefore, have used the IJAAF design. However, the long-running institutional rivalry between the two services blocked this. The IJNAAF wanted its own design.

To compensate for naval limitation treaty restrictions on ships during the interwar period, the IJN had instructed the IJNAF to develop long-range, land-based torpedo-bombers. The Mitsubishi G3M was the first such aircraft to reach operational units, from 1936, followed by the company's G4M in 1941. Both aircraft had a range of more than 3,000 miles. When the G3M entered service, the standard IJNAF fighter of the period, the Mitsubishi A5M, had a maximum range of 745 miles. Its replacement, the superlative A6M Zero-sen, could cover 1,930 miles. Clearly, the IJNAF needed a dedicated land-based fighter escort to accompany its long-range bombers.

In June 1938 the IJNAF instructed Mitsubishi and Nakajima to each develop a heavy fighter along the lines of the Bf 110. It was to be a twin-engined aircraft with a

The redesigned J1N1-C prototype was completely unarmed, as befitted its new-found role as a reconnaissance aircraft after the original J1N1 heavy fighter was abandoned by the IJNAF. This particular airframe was one of a handful of nearly completed examples that Nakajima was authorized to modify on the assembly line to serve as prototypes for fast, land-based long-range reconnaissance aircraft. Some of these later become nightfighters with 251st Kokutai after further modification. (US Navy)

crew of three. Both companies began working on designs, although Mitsubishi soon withdrew from the project due to existing commitments. The Nakajima aircraft, designated the J1N, finally flew for the first time on May 2, 1941.

Like the Ki-45, the aircraft initially proved inadequate due to it being underpowered. The prototype mounted four of its six 7.7mm Type 97 machine guns in two remotely controlled barbettes on the fuselage behind the pilot's cockpit. Two other Type 97s, along with a single 20mm Type 99 cannon, were housed in the nose, firing forward. The weaponry installed in the "heavy" fighter provided the J1N with less firepower than the A6M single-engined fighter.

The prototype was plagued with teething troubles throughout its flight trials, pilots complaining of sluggish handling and inadequate power from the aircraft's Nakajima Sakae radial engines. A second prototype was fitted with trailing-edge flaps and leading-edge slots, which improved the J1N1's maneuverability. Both aircraft were delivered to the IJNAF for service trials in August 1941. The latter proved to be disastrous because the J1N1 was considerably overweight, suffered from hydraulic problems and was beset with severe aileron vibration during rolls. Furthermore, the barbettes were difficult to aim effectively, and they were too heavy. Despite the fighter's maneuverability drawing praise, the J1N1 was outperformed by an A6M2 Zero-sen in comparative trials. This led to the IJNAF rejecting the aircraft as a long-range escort fighter in October 1941.

Noting that the J1N1 was almost as quick as a Zero-sen, the IJNAF authorized Nakajima to modify airframes nearing completion on the assembly line to serve as prototypes for a long-range reconnaissance aircraft. This involved stripping the aircraft of much of its armament, reducing fuel capacity, improving engine reliability, and redesigning the fuselage to accommodate a forward cockpit for the pilot and radio/operator gunner, and a separate cockpit located behind the trailing edge of the wing for the navigator/observer. Given the designation J1N1-C, the first three examples of what was codenamed the "Irving" by the Allies made their combat debut from Rabaul in July 1942.

By then, aerial combat in war-torn Europe had long since exposed the twin-engined heavy fighter's inadequacies. Lacking sufficient speed and agility to defeat single-engined opponents in the skies over France and England during 1940, the Bf 110 had quickly been removed from its intended role of fighter escort for the Luftwaffe's large medium bomber force. Despite this, the IJAAF initially persisted with using its Ki-45s as bomber escorts in Burma and China from the fall of 1942. Like the Bf 110s some two years earlier, they proved unable to defend vulnerable medium bombers from attack by single-engined Allied fighters.

Although inadequate as bomber escorts, the Japanese twin-engined fighters showed promise as bomber interceptors. The USAAF's B-17 and B-24 had proven to be formidable opponents for Japan's single-engined fighters, which were typically armed with two 7.7mm machine guns and two 20mm cannon or four 12.7mm machine guns. Such weaponry frequently proved to be too light to bring down the well-armed, and armored, American heavy bombers.

Maneuverability was less of a factor for bomber interceptors. Twin-engined fighters could carry heavier weapons than their single-engined counterparts. As bomber interceptors, Ki-45s were rearmed with two nose-mounted 12.7mm Ho-103 machine

36ft 1in.

49ft 3in.

guns and, eventually, a forward-firing, hand-loaded 37mm Type 98 cannon in a ventral tunnel. The later dedicated nightfighter variant (Ki-45 KAIc) featured a semi-automatic 37mm Ho-203 cannon in the nose and two obliquely firing 20mm Ho-5 cannon in the center fuselage, but with the fighter's pointed nose left devoid of armament because it was meant to house radar equipment then under development.

Following a series of effective night attacks by USAAF heavy bombers on the IJN's Rabaul bases from the summer/fall of 1942, the IJNAF became painfully aware it was powerless to stop such raids. A night interceptor was urgently needed. A6M-equipped 251st Kokutai, led by Cdr Yasuna Kozono, was given the task of repelling night

attacks upon its return to Rabaul in May 1943 following reequipment in Japan. Aside from 58 A6M3 Zero-sen, the unit was also issued with two J1N1-Cs – a third was subsequently ferried to Rabaul. With the latter aircraft's arrival in-theater, Kozono ordered that the J1N1-C be field-fitted with ventral and dorsal Type 99 20mm cannon firing upward and downward at 30 degrees.

This modification had been undertaken after Kozono had presented the concept of a suitably modified J1N1-C sneaking up and attacking an enemy bomber undetected at night to a planning board meeting held at the Aeronautics Section of the Department of the Navy in Yokosuka on November 20, 1942. The presentation culminated with a fist-pounding Kozono being turned down by the board. He persisted, nevertheless, and a combination of his bullying, cooperative technical personnel and subsequent practical success resulted in the conversion of a handful of J1N1-C airframes held by the Yokosuka Air Arsenal into nightfighters.

In May–June 1943, the solitary modified J1N1-C nightfighter that had originally been converted by 251st Kokutai was joined by several more modified aircraft from Yokosuka – one of the makeshift nightfighters was written off in a landing accident en route to Rabaul, however. Kozono's innovation quickly proved successful, with PO1c Shigetoshi Kudo downing two B-17Es sent to bomb Rabaul on the night of May 21, 1943. Further victories followed shortly thereafter, and in July 251st Kokutai sent "Irving" nightfighter detachments further afield to Buin, Buka and Ballale.

The IJNAF's Naval Staff quickly took note of the success enjoyed by 251st Kokutai, ordering Nakajima to produce a dedicated nightfighter version of the aircraft as the J1N1-S. Until this aircraft went into production, the IJNAF had to make do with converting reconnaissance J1N1-Cs into nightfighters by fitting them with two obliquely firing cannon – the resulting aircraft was redesignated the J1N1-C KAI. To provide room for these guns, the navigator's position was removed, making the nightfighter a two-man aircraft. To reflect its new role, the IJNAF named the aircraft Gekko (Moonlight).

This field-modified J1N1-C was the third such aircraft assigned to 251st Kokutai, and it is seen here taxiing at Vunakanau during trials undertaken by FCPO Shigetoshi Kudo in May 1943. It had recently been fitted with obliquely firing dorsal and ventral 20mm cannon at Lakunai, turning the previously unarmed reconnaissance aircraft into a nightfighter. (Michael Claringbould Collection)

OPPOSITE

Adorned with a distinctive yellow unit marking on its fin and rudder, this Toryu was assigned to 53rd Sentai's 3rd Hikotai in the spring of 1945. At that time, the unit was flying from Matsudo, less than 15 miles northeast of central Tokyo. It had been transferred here in August 1944, three months after forming at nearby Tokorozawa – recognized as the birthplace of Japanese aviation. 53rd Sentai was exclusively equipped with the Ki-45 KAI, and its crews were credited with no fewer than 168 B-29s destroyed or damaged between November 1944 and July 1945

The definitive J1N1-S featured a redesigned upper fuselage that eliminated the step between the rear of the observer's cockpit and the base of the vertical fin. Individual exhaust stacks were also fitted in place of the collector ring. Combat experience with the J1N1-S saw crews report that the downward-firing cannon were less effective than the upward-firing weapons. The former were replaced by two nose-mounted 20mm cannon in the J1N1-Sa. The latter aircraft also had a third obliquely firing cannon, with some examples featuring air intercept (AI) radar and associated antennas installed in the nose instead of the cannon from 1945, and others boasting a searchlight.

The makeshift IJAAF and IJNAF nightfighters of 1943–44 lacked radar, forcing pilots and their gunners to locate their quarry visually. Initially, the IJNAF had fitted its J1N1-Cs with spotlights aimed upward to illuminate targets, but their operational usefulness was questionable – turning them on before firing warned the target aircraft it was under attack.

While the Allies and Germany equipped their nightfighters with radar from 1941–42, Japan's development of such equipment lagged. The postwar US Naval Technical Mission to Japan determined that the IJAAF and the IJNAF had only two effective nightfighter AI radars at war's end. Neither was in production, with each set having to be manufactured individually. The IJNAF introduced its FD-2 AI radar in August 1944, installing the system in aircraft as sets became available, but only if pilots wanted them. The IJAAF's Gyuku-3 radar came along still later. It was supposed to be installed in the Ki-45, but few, if any, were. Both sets were unreliable, being prone to failure. Pilots did not understand radar's utility, viewing the sets as unnecessary weight – they often stripped their aircraft of everything except the guns and radio in order to improve speed and performance.

PO1c Shigetoshi Kudo of 251st Kokutai was Japan's first nighfighter ace, claiming six B-17Es and a B-24D destroyed while flying converted J1N1-Cs in defense of Rabaul from Lakunai. Subsequent successes operating from Ballale, in the Solomon Islands, took his tally to eight destroyed in two months. Returning to Japan in February 1944 and posted to Yokosuka Kokutai, Kudo failed to add to his total. (Tony Holmes Collection)

This damaged J1N1-Sa of 302nd Kokutai was found at Kisarazu Naval Air Base, in Chiba Prefecture, in late September 1945. The barrels for the nightfighter's three obliquely-mounted Type 99 20mm cannon can be seen in the upper fuselage aft of the rear cockpit. This aircraft lacks the antenna array for the FD-2 AI radar that was installed in a number of late-build Gekkos, the nightfighter instead featuring a glazed nose cone possibly covering a searchlight. (National Archives and Records Administration)

TECHNICAL SPECIFICATIONS

B-29 SUPERFORTRESS

STRUCTURE

The B-29's structure was unique among World War II bombers, not just in terms of its size, but also in the elements of its construction. The aircraft's aerodynamics were unprecedented, it had pressurized cabins, an innovative control system and tricycle landing gear. The B-29 represented the leading edge of aeronautical engineering in the mid-1940s.

Boeing had paid unusual attention to the design's aerodynamics. The fuselage, wings and appendages were designed in such a way that drag was kept to a minimum. Protrusions, including the gun turrets, were reduced in size and streamlined. Furthermore, skin panels were butt-seamed and the skin attached with countersunk flush-head rivets. The fuselage cross-section was circular throughout, with no discontinuities. It had a cylindrical body that tapered into a semispherical nose. The wing combined a high coefficient of lift with low drag. The aircraft's structure combined unprecedented strength with flexibility, allowing a wing loading of 69lb per square feet – double that of the B-17 and 50 percent greater than the B-24.

A monocoque structure, it achieved maximum strength at minimum weight through a combination of internal framing and thick skin. Longitudinal frames on the

fuselage were eight inches apart. The skin was the thickest used to date on an aircraft – on both the fuselage and inner wing it was 0.1875in. thick. Wing spars were similarly robust, with their flanges weighing 255lb. The wings had a 4.5-degree dihedral and a seven-degree leading edge sweep-back, which improved stability.

The fuselage consisted of five major assemblies – the forward pressurized compartment, the bomb-bays, the wing gap closure, the aft section (with pressurized and unpressurized compartments), and the tail gunner's compartment. The mid-section (with the bomb-bays and wing gap closure) and the rear half of the aft section were unpressurized. The forward and aft compartments and the tail gunner's compartment were all pressurized. The wing had three major assemblies – the inboard wing, which ran from the starboard to port outer engine nacelle, and two outer wings, port and starboard. These were made by subcontractors at various major B-29 assembly plants.

The forward pressurized compartment accommodated both pilots and the bombardier, navigator, radio operator, and flight engineer. The aft pressurized compartment was where three gunners were stationed, and it also contained the toilet and bunks. The rear compartment housed the tail gunner. To allow travel between the forward and aft pressurized compartments, a pressurized tunnel ran the length of the bomb-bay. Movement between the tail gunner's compartment and the aft pressurized compartment could only be undertaken when the bomber was depressurized. Cabins were equipped with sound-dampening and temperature-insulating fiberglass blankets.

Superchargers maintained a cabin pressure of 8,000ft up to 30,000ft in these compartments, and an air conditioning system heated or chilled the air to 70°F. The cabin was depressurized 30 minutes prior to combat, cooling the cabin temperature. When depressurization began, the crew donned oxygen masks to breath and plug-in flight suit heaters to stay warm. Smoking was allowed when the aircraft was pressurized.

ENGINES

The B-29 was powered by four 18-cylinder Wright R-3350 Duplex-Cyclone radial engines. Each powerplant had two rows of nine cylinders set radially around a central axis. Each cylinder had a 6.125in. diameter and a 6.3125in. stroke. Total engine displacement was 3,347.9 cubic inches. The R-3350 had a pushrod drivetrain and was equipped with a two-speed single-stage turbo-supercharger. The dry weight of the engine was 2,670lb. It burned either 100 or 130 octane aviation gasoline.

Generating 2,200hp in the version fitted to the B-29 during World War II, the R-3350 was one the conflict's most powerful aircraft engines. Its development had started in January 1936, in part as a response to the competing Pratt & Whitney R-2800 Double Wasp. A prototype of the R-3350 was first run in May 1937, but progress was slow over the next two years. Wright delivered only seven engines to the USAAC for ground-running between 1936–39.

Development accelerated after the USAAC released the RFP for a "super bomber" in December 1939. The performance required by the USAAC dictated the creation of an engine capable of producing more than 2,000hp. The only powerplant meeting this requirement was the R-3350, which had not yet flown – the first examples to take to the air were pre-production engines installed in the XB-19 in June 1941. All four bomber designs submitted in response to the RFP specified the R-3350 for their engines.

Wright received its first production order for the R-3350 in May 1941, but design changes, low manufacturing priority, and factory limitations meant the first examples were not delivered until year-end. Following the attack on Pearl Harbor, and with the USAAF's growing interest in the "super bomber," Wright received better financial support for engine construction. It duly built a factory in Woodbridge, New Jersey, and established an R-3350 production line. A second line was set up in its Cincinnati plant after production of its other engines was moved elsewhere. Manufacturing was also contracted to Chrysler in 1942, which built a factory in Chicago and commenced the construction of 10,000 R-3350s.

Despite these measures, full production was not reached until 1944. This meant the R-3350 was being developed concurrently with the bombers that intended to use it. The Duplex-Cyclone represented as big an advance in aircraft engine technology as the B-29 did in aeronautical technology. Like the bomber it was supposed to power, the engine had numerous technical faults that needed to be overcome. Problems were compounded by workforce inexperience, with most production line workers being as new to aviation manufacturing as the engines they were building.

Virtually everything that could go wrong did. Early engines burned excessive oil, reduction gear failures were common, the carburetors required redesigning and the engines ran so hot they frequently caught fire. The crankcase contained metallic magnesium, which an engine fire could ignite. When that happened, the heat of the fire was so great it would burn through the main wing spar. Often, this took just seconds, resulting in a catastrophic wing failure. Ultimately, a cowling redesign mitigated overheating issues.

These problems were eventually fixed, but not until January 1945 were the engines truly reliable. Although they could still burst into flames if the

The Wright R-3350 Duplex-Cyclone was one of the breakthrough pieces of technology used on the B-29. Amongst the most powerful piston engines built for aircraft during World War II, the Duplex-Cyclone was still under development when chosen for the Superfortress. It was well after the B-29 was in service before all the engine's bugs were resolved. (NMAF)

crew abused them, the R-3350s no longer ignited. As assembly line workers and aircrew mastered the learning curves in manufacturing and operating the engine, the Duplex-Cyclone finally delivered dependable performance.

ARMAMENT

The B-29 was one of the most heavily armed bombers of World War II, originally being equipped with 12 0.50-cal. AN/M2 Browning machine guns and one 20mm M2 cannon (the US Army and the US Navy used identical weapons, especially for aircraft, with commonality being indicated by the designation "AN" for Army–Navy). Ten of the 0.50-cal. machine guns were in unmanned, remotely controlled General Electric power turrets. Two 0.50-cal. machine guns and the sole 20mm cannon were in a manned position in the tail. Both weapons were air-cooled, and mechanically reliable.

The B-29 had remotely controlled power turrets operated through the Central Station Fire Control System. The side gunner aimed the turret(s) under control using the gunsight he is seen operating here. During night missions the gunners usually served as observers, for their weapons (bar the tail turret) were unloaded. (NMAF)

The M2 was a US licensed version of the Hispano-Suiza HS.404 Mk II 20mm cannon. With a muzzle velocity of 2,800ft per second, it fired a 4.6oz projectile (armor-piercing, high-explosive or incendiary), with a rate of fire of 700 to 750 rounds per minute. The high-explosive round charge was between 0.21–0.39oz. The AN/M2 0.50-cal. fired a 52-gram bullet with a muzzle velocity of 2,910ft per second. Capable of expending 750–850 rounds per minute, the AN/M2 was particularly effective against lightly armored Japanese fighters – its rounds could penetrate one inch of armor.

The B-29 had front upper, aft upper, front lower and aft lower turrets. The front upper turret had four 0.50-cal. machine guns, while the rest had two each. They were operated by three gunners (upper, right and left) and the bombardier. The gunners occupied sighting stations located at Plexiglas blisters in the middle of the fuselage. The turrets were operated using the General Electric Central Station Fire Control System. It allowed any gunner to operate all the turrets, or just their primary station. The bombardier had primary control of both forward turrets. The upper gunner had primary control of the aft turret and secondary control of the front turret. The waist gunners split primary control of the lower aft turret and secondary control of the lower front turret. The tail gunner fired the tail turret guns.

Gunners used a reflector sight connected to a gunnery computer which set the attacking aircraft's wingspan and tracked it. This was fed into a computer, which took the observations, combined them with information provided by the navigator (airspeed and

B-29 SUPERFORTRESS TURRET

B-29s were equipped with four remotely controlled General Electric power turrets mounting ten 0.50-cal. Browning AN/M2 machine guns. The bomber was fitted with three twin-gun turrets (illustrated) and one four-gun turret. The air-cooled AN/M2 was very reliable, had a high rate of fire, and fired rounds capable of penetrating an inch of steel.

Although each remotely controlled turret was capable of carrying 500 rounds of ammunition per gun, their magazines were usually left empty during night missions, with the B-29 relying on speed (and the armed and manned rear turret) for defense.

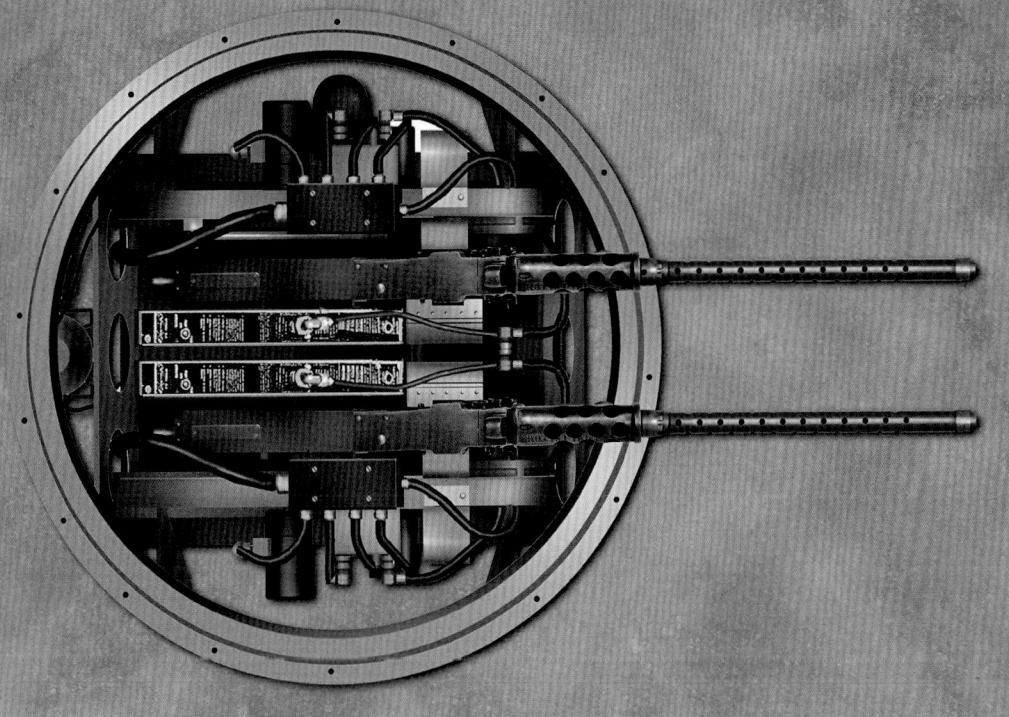

atmospheric data) and aimed the gun turrets, correcting for lead, parallax, windage and bullet drop. The system worked well.

On night raids, frequently no ammunition for the guns was carried. On the first night raids, only the lower turrets were armed. After experience showed night attacks almost always came from behind, all turrets were left unloaded except for the tail guns. Early detection of attacking nightfighters proved more important than ammunition. A B-29 could outrun both the Ki-45 and the J1N1 if they were spotted before an attack, the flight engineer opening the throttles and leaving the bomber's opponent unable to catch the fleeing Superfortress. Usually, the upper, right and left gunners flew night missions even when their weapons were empty, serving as lookouts.

ELECTRONICS

The B-29 carried the most sophisticated electronic suite of any aircraft in World War II. Although designed before AI radar and electronic countermeasures (ECM) existed, the aircraft had sufficient volume and carrying capacity that these could easily be added as retrofitted equipment. Much of the bomber's electronics were installed during the manufacturing process, rather than as field modifications. This improved reliability.

OPPOSITE

A posed photograph of a factory-fresh B-29 showing the upper rear turret and blister position. This was the Central Station Fire Control System commander's position, and with a 360-degree view, he was responsible for assigning the individual turrets to the other gunners when needed. During daylight missions, each gun would have been provided with 500 rounds of ammunition. (Tony Holmes Collection)

The B-29 carried an SRC-269 radio compass, AN/APQ-4 navigation system, SCR-695 radio identification system, RC-43A marker beacon receiver, SRC-570 landing guidance system, AN/ARN-7 radar compass, AN/APQ-13 or AN/APQ-7 navigation and bombing radar, and an SCR-729 or AN/APN-2 radar interrogation system. It could also be equipped with AN/APQ-9 and AN/APR-4 radar jammers and the AN/APT-1 airborne radar warning system.

The navigation equipment permitted the B-29 to accurately reach its target and then return safely home despite flying nearly 1,500 miles each way. The SCR-269 radio compass gave greater accuracy than the standard magnetic compass. The AN/APQ-4 used broadcast signals to fix the position of an aircraft – postwar, it became the Long-Range Navigation (LORAN) system. The AN/APQ-4 worked up to 1,500 miles from the ground broadcast station (roughly the distance from Saipan to Tokyo), with an accuracy of tens of miles. The AN/ARN-7 was a radar that could be used for homing. The AN/APQ-13 was an advanced navigation and bombing radar. An improvement of the H2X (AN/APS-15) radar, it increased bombing accuracy enough to justify redesigning the B-29 to allow it to become standard equipment. The radar allowed blind bombing of city-sized targets. The AN/APQ-7 improved accuracy still further, permitting precise radar bombing of large facilities like oil refineries and shipyards.

The various ECM systems aboard the B-29 were used to jam ground-based early warning and gunnery radars. AN/APQ-9 was a barrage jamming set effective against gun-laying and tracking radars. This was supplemented by the AN/APR-4 for spot jamming. It used an AN/APT-1 search receiver to locate an enemy radar set, which

The AN/ARN-7 radar compass was part of the electronics suite carried by the B-29. An airborne direction finder, it aided the bombers' return to base after a mission. This card, once classified restricted, provides instructional information on the unit to its operators. (Author's Collection)

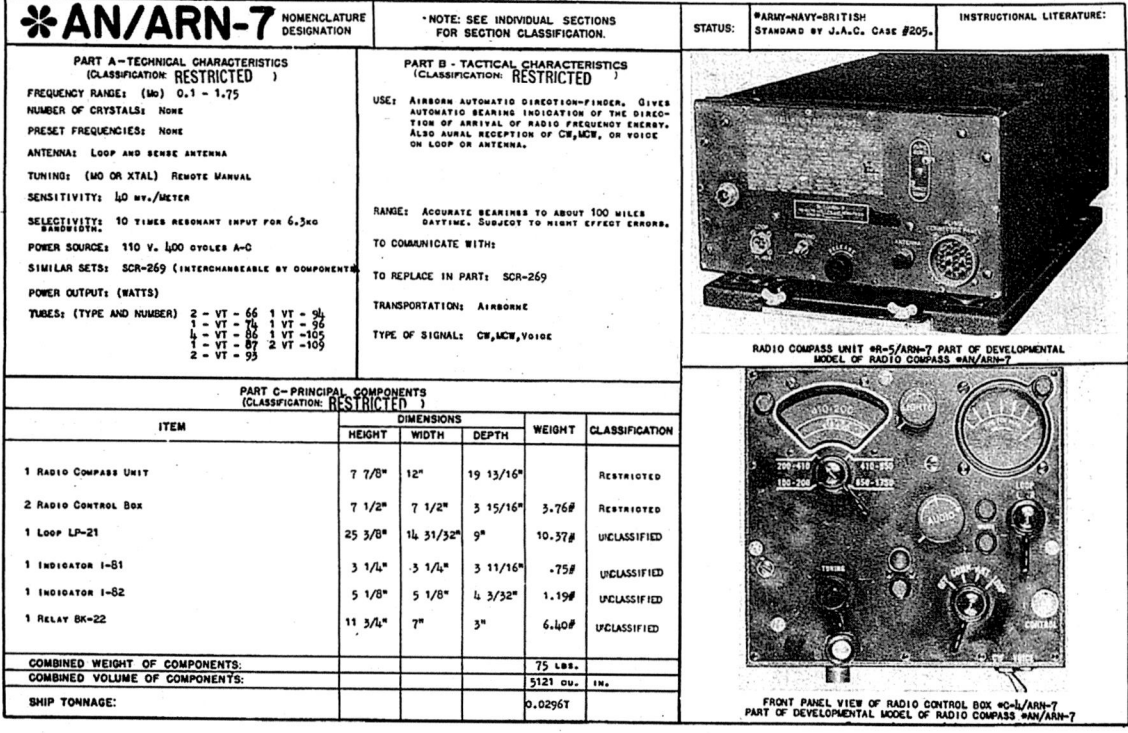

would then be jammed by a focused signal from the AN/APR-4. The combination of barrage and spot jamming was so effective that the Japanese began turning off their equipment when jamming began. This ECM gear was carried on specially outfitted bombers called "Ravens" or "Guardian Angels," with four such aircraft being assigned to each wing.

Due to the frequencies used by Japanese radars, the short-length chaff dropped in Europe was useless. Instead, 6in. x 400ft strips of metal foil known as "rope" were used. While effective, bombers could not carry much when fully loaded with ordnance. Often, the ECM-equipped "Guardian Angels" carried "rope" instead of bombs to increase jamming capacity.

Most of the electronics aboard the B-29 related to navigation, targeting or countermeasures against ground radar. It made the Superfortress a more effective bomber, but was useless as a defense against nightfighters. B-29s did not carry radar capable of detecting other aircraft. The only electronic tool available was the AN/APT-1, which detected radar signals, including AI systems. Since most Japanese nightfighters did not carry radar, its protection could be illusionary. The absence of a warning did not mean there were no enemy aircraft close enough to attack, only that there were no Japanese nightfighters using radar nearby.

JAPANESE NIGHTFIGHTER

STRUCTURE

The Ki-45 and the J1N1 were similar in construction and appearance. Both were twin-engined monoplanes of all-metal construction with fabric-covered control surfaces. They had a single fuselage with a conventional rudder and horizontal stabilizer. Both had engines located in conventional nacelles roughly one-quarter of the distance to the wingtip. Both had a conventional undercarriage, with retractable

A Ki-45 KAIc, fitted with two obliquely firing 20mm Ho-5 cannon in the center fuselage, is parked at Clark Field, near Manila, ahead of a Ki-45 KAIa, a Mitsubishi Ki-46 "Dinah" and a J1N1-S in February 1945, by which point the airfield was under USAAF control. The designs of all three twin-engined types seen here dated back to the latter half of the 1930s. They represented aeronautical thinking at the transition point between biplanes and monoplanes and the wood-and-canvas aircraft of preceding years and the metal framed and covered types of World War II. (Tony Holmes Collection)

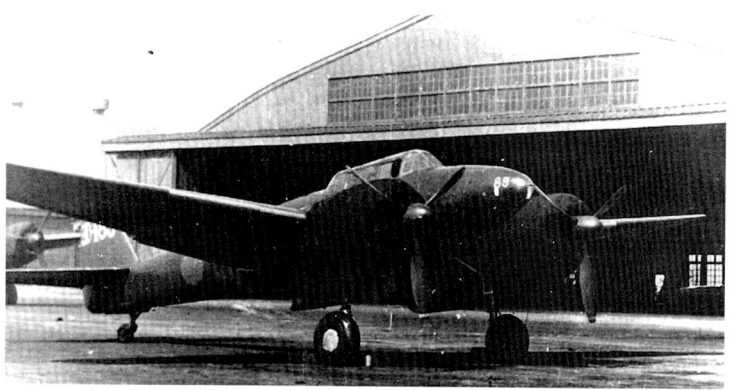

Lacking FD-2 AI radar and also possibly armament, a J1N1-S of 302nd Kokutai sits on the ramp at Atsugi in 1944–45. This unit also flew a handful of Yokosuka P1Y1 Ginga and D4Y2-S Suisei as makeshift nightfighters, although neither type proved successful when it came to repelling B-29 raids. (Tony Holmes Collection)

main gear – they belonged to the first generation of Japanese aircraft with retractable landing gear. Getting the undercarriage to work reliably was one of the factors that delayed the appearance of both aircraft. Despite their conventional construction, such innovations delayed getting a finished design into service.

When the Ki-45 started flight testing, it failed to meet expectations. The primary culprit was nacelle drag, which proved much larger than expected. The aircraft had to be fitted with propeller spinners and closer-fitting cowlings in an attempt to rectify this problem. Although they reduced drag, the spinners and cowlings constrained airflow to the engine cylinders, which led to the air-cooled nine-cylinder Nakajima Ha-20b radials overheating. Ducted spinners which forced cooling air to the engines were added. In April 1940, Kawasaki was instructed by the IJAAF to fit more powerful 14-cylinder Nakajima Ha-25 engines in place of the Ha-20bs.

Similar problems plagued the development of the J1N1. When the first prototype was found to lack maneuverability, leading edge slots and trailing edge flaps that could be deployed in combat and during landing were added to the wings. The aircraft was initially fitted with two tandem-mounted remotely controlled barbettes, each armed with two 7.7mm machine guns, atop the fuselage behind the cockpit. However, they proved difficult to aim and were too heavy, adding to the J1N1's weight-related performance problems. In mock dogfights with the A6M2 Zero-sen, the heavy fighter proved inferior (with or without the barbettes), resulting in its rejection by the IJNAF in its designed role.

Ironically, the J1N1's transformation into a long-range reconnaissance aircraft made it an ideal candidate for nightfighter conversion. All armament was removed and weight-saving measures improved its speed. Replacing the observer with obliquely-firing 20mm guns was simply done in an airframe of that size. As need for a nightfighter grew, the IJNAF had an obvious candidate.

The problem for both the Ki-45 and the J1N1 lay in their long gestation. Both were designs from the mid-1930s – the opening of a transitional period in aircraft design. By the time they entered service, the aircraft had been outclassed in their intended roles by the next generation of fighters. Both were pressed into service as nightfighters because nothing better was available to the Japanese. As nightfighters, they proved adequate against the B-17 and B-24. However, their main opponent in Japan, the B-29, was a generation ahead of those early-war four-engined bombers. The Superfortress was faster than the Ki-45 and the J1N1, had a better performance at high altitude, and was structurally stronger.

ENGINES

Both Japanese nightfighters were twin-engined, with the Ki-45s used in this role being powered by two Mitsubishi Ha-102s each rated at 1,080hp for takeoff – this powerplant was primarily used by IJAAF aircraft in World War II. The J1N1 was fitted with two Nakajima NK1F Sakae 21s. Both were air-cooled radial engines with 14 cylinders arranged in two rows of seven cylinders.

The Ha-102 was the older design. It first appeared in 1931 as the Ha-26, or Zuisei 11 (for the IJNAF), and the Type 99 radial Model 2 (for the IJAAF). Each cylinder, which had a 5.5in. bore and a 5.12in. stroke, displaced two liters for a total displacement of 28 liters. The Ha-102 had a pushrod-operated valve train and burned 87 octane gasoline. Weighing 1,190lb, the original version produced 875hp at 2,540 rpm on takeoff and 925hp at 2,450rpm at 5,900ft.

The Ki-45 KAIc nightfighter was fitted with an uprated version of the Ha-102, with a two-stage supercharger. The latter allowed the engine to run at a faster rpm with greater power. At 2,700rpm it produced 1,080hp on takeoff and 1,055hp at 9,185ft. Power fell away at high altitudes, however. At 19,000ft each engine generated 950hp, and this figure steadily dropped as the Ki-45 climbed. It took a skilled pilot to keep an aircraft with Ha-102s from stalling at 30,000ft.

The engines fitted to the J1N1-C/S nightfighter were also underpowered particularly at higher altitudes. Some sources state that the Nakajima NK1F Sakae 21 was a development of the company's earlier Ha-5 (Army Type 97) 850hp radial engine, which appeared in 1933. Other sources state it was developed from the French Gnome-Rhône 14K, built under license in Japan. Regardless of the engine's origins, the N1KF was a significant improvement over either the Ha-5 or the Gnome-Rhône 14K. Its cylinders had a bore of 5.12in. and a 5.9in. stroke, yielding a cylinder displacement of 1.99 liters – a total displacement of 27.9 liters. The engine ran on 92 octane gasoline and weighed 1,300lb.

The N1KF had an overhead valve train and a gear-driven two-speed supercharger. Producing 1,130hp on takeoff, 1,100hp at 9,350ft and 980hp at 19,700ft, the engine's performance also fell off dramatically above 19,000ft. Capable of flying reliably at very lean fuel mixtures, thus permitting extended cruising range, the N1KF was widely used. It was most famously fitted to the A6M3/5 Zero-sen.

The engines that powered the Ki-45 and J1N1 were prewar designs, analogous to the Pratt & Whitney R-1830 Twin Wasp fitted to the Wildcat fighter and C-47 Skytrain transport or the Bristol Hercules III used by the Wellington bomber. They were all outclassed by the next generation of aircraft engines such as the Pratt & Whitney R-2800 Double Wasp, produced in 1,500hp and 2,000hp versions. The Wright R-3350-23 Duplex-Cyclone used by the B-29 was even more powerful, being rated at 2,200hp. This meant that crews flying Ki-45 KAIc and J1N1-C/S nightfighters faced an opponent that was four times the size and six times the weight of their aircraft, yet was ten percent faster.

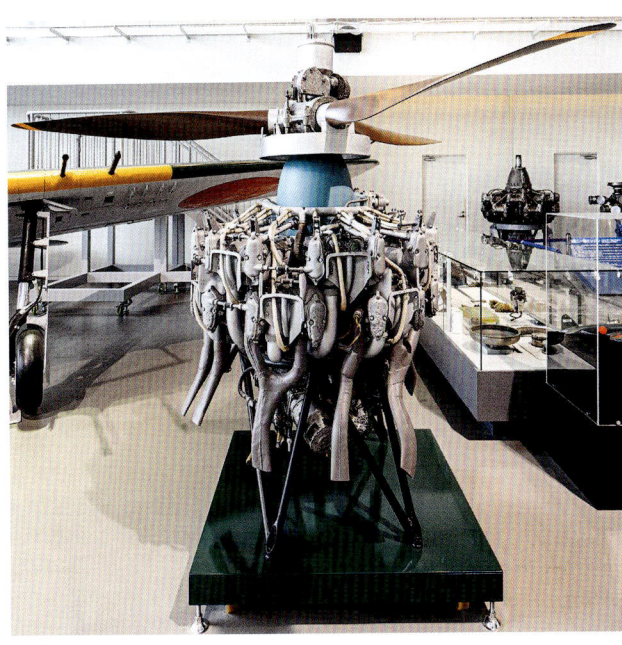

The production version of the J1N1 used a pair of Nakajima NK1F Sakae 21 radials for propulsion, this engine also being fitted to the A6M3/5 Zero-sen. While state of the art when introduced, and effective during the early years of the Pacific War, the NK1F had been outclassed by 1944. (Wikimedia)

Ho-203 37mm CANNON

The Ki-45 KAIc was equipped with a nose-mounted Ho-203 37mm cannon, developed from the Year 11 Type infantry gun. Featuring a 15-round magazine, the weapon (which was 60.3 in. in length and weighed 196lb) fired a 1.04lb explosive round that was effective over a distance of 2,950ft.

The Ki-45 KAIc carried a 37mm Ho-203 cannon in either a pod under the belly or (in nightfighter versions) mounted in the nose. It had a cylindrical magazine that held 15 rounds. The gunner changed magazines when the weapon was belly mounted, but it was up to the pilot to do this with a nose-mounted gun as seen here – a difficult undertaking at night. (Author's Collection)

ARMAMENT

As nightfighters, the Ki-45 KAIc and J1N1-C/S depended on their guns to down B-29s. The Toryu was armed with a single 37mm Ho-203 and two 20mm Ho-5 cannon. The Gekko used the 20mm Type 99 cannon. The various air-to-air bombs, parachute bombs and incendiaries developed to down B-29s were not used by nightfighters. The Toryu also carried a flexibly mounted 7.92mm machine gun, but this was primarily for defense against Allied fighters attacking from the rear. Using it against a B-29 at night would have been counterproductive, for it was too light to cause serious damage to the bomber and firing the machine gun would have warned the bomber's crew of the nightfighter's presence.

The Ho-203 was a 37mm cannon used by the IJAAF. Developed from the Year 11 Type infantry gun, it had a 15-round drum and fired a 1.04lb explosive round. Against most aircraft, one hit would result in a kill. The semi-automatic weapon was installed in the ventral tunnel on the starboard side of the fuselage, firing forward (with the gunner replacing spent magazines).

The Ho-5 was a 20mm autocannon developed from the Ho-3. The lightweight weapon was similar in construction to the 12.7mm Ho-103 Type 1 machine gun, which in turn was similar in design and operation to the Browning AN/M2 0.50-cal. weapon. Using disintegrating

Ho-5 20mm CANNON

The Ho-5 20mm autocannon was directly developed from the Ho-103 Type 1 12.7mm machine gun (which was in turn similar to the AN/M2 0.50.cal. weapon). One of the most effective guns fielded by IJAAF aircraft, it featured a 50-round drum in the Ki-45 KAIc. The Ho-5 fired a 0.361lb round, which could be explosive (most commonly used), incendiary or solid.

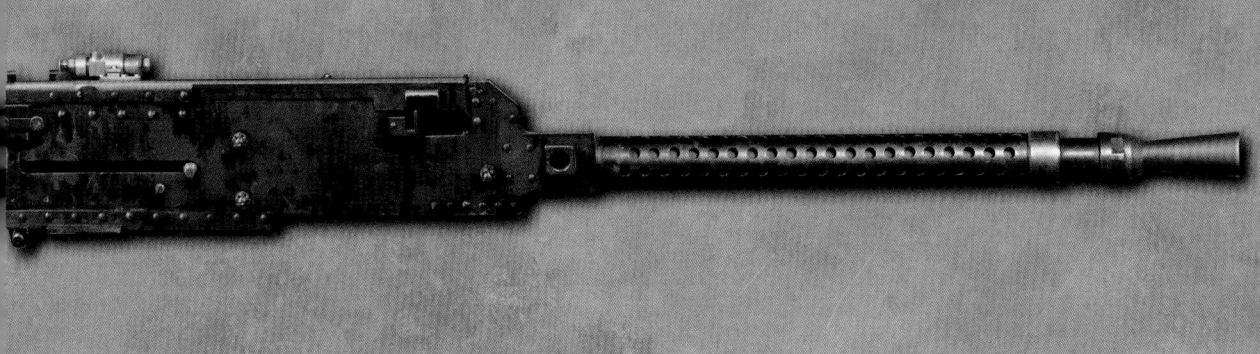

metal link belts for the ammunition, the Ho-5 was one of the best aircraft weapons fielded by the Japanese. It featured a 50-round drum in the Ki-45 KAIc, which could be replaced by the gunner when expended. The Ho-5 fired a 0.361lb round, which could be explosive (most commonly used), incendiary or solid. Nightfighter conversions of the Ki-45 featured two Ho-5s installed between the gunner and pilot firing obliquely up at an angle of 30 degrees.

J1N1-C/S nightfighters were armed exclusively with the 20mm Type 99 cannon, which was a licence-built version of the Oerlikon FF 20mm autocannon. There were two versions produced in Japan, the Mk 1 and the longer-barreled Mk 2, which fired the same projectile, although the Mk 2 had a larger cartridge. The combination of more propellant and a longer barrel gave the Mk 2 a higher rate of fire and greater muzzle velocity than the Mk 1. It also weighed more than the Type 99-1. The Gekko was probably equipped with both marks during its career as a nightfighter, as early examples were conversions that used whatever guns were at hand. As the war progressed, the Mk 2 became favored due to its greater muzzle energy. The J1N1-C/Ss facing B-29s in 1944–45 most likely mounted Type 99-2s. Although the weapon could be either belt or drum fed, the IJNAF preferred the latter. It normally installed 50- or 100-round drums in the Gekko nightfighter.

Gun mounting varied. Early examples of the J1N1-C had four 20mm weapons, two firing obliquely up and two firing obliquely down, both at an angle of 30 degrees. Later conversions (J1N1-S) mounted two 20mm cannon in fixed mountings firing obliquely up at an angle of 30 degrees. As the war progressed, a final arrangement of three upward-firing guns was adopted (late-build J1N1-S). These were fed by 100-round drums, which could be replaced by the gunner when exhausted. Neither the Toryu nor the Gekko were initially built with obliquely firing weapons. These were all added as field modifications once the aircraft reached its operational station. If a Ki-45 was intended for use exclusively as a daytime bomber interceptor, the obliquely-firing guns were omitted, as they added 150–200kg to the aircraft's weight and could not be used in daytime attacks.

Ki-45 TORYU Ho-5 20mm CANNON

This cutaway shows the standard fitment for the obliquely-mounted Ho-5 20mm guns installed in the Ki-45 KAIc – the IJNAF's J1N1-C KAI and some J1N1-Ss had a similar arrangement, but with Type 99 20mm cannon instead. In the Toryu, the Ho-5s were fixed in a pedestal mounting placed between the pilot and observer/gunner. Both weapons were seated so that they fired at a 30-degree angle above the nose. The guns were fed by magazines containing 200 20mm rounds in total, with spent casings being ejected into a tray directly below the cannon. In the Ki-45 KAIc, the observer could service the guns in flight, charging them and clearing jams if required.

1. Twin obliquely mounted Ho-5 20mm cannon
2. Fuel-filling tube
3. Fuel tank
4. Ammunition magazines
5. Spent ammunition link chute to storage tray
6. Port cannon mounting
7. Oxygen bottles
8. Pilot's 0.37in. head armor
9. Pilot's seat

ELECTRONICS

While the B-29 and its crew had numerous electronic devices to aid them in their missions, their counterparts in Japanese nightfighters were less fortunate. In fact the only electronics aboard a typical IJAAF or IJNAF nightfighter was its radio. Very few were outfitted with radar. In the few cases where AI radar was installed, the units used were unreliable. Furthermore, the crews were poorly trained in their employment and mistrusted their effectiveness.

Type 99 20mm CANNON

All J1N1 nightfighters relied on the Type 99 20mm cannon, typically four in number (two firing obliquely up and two firing obliquely down, both at an angle of 30 degrees). A licence-built version of the Oerlikon FF 20mm autocannon, the Type 99 was available in short-barrel Mk 1 or longer-barrel Mk 2 models. They were installed in a variety of ways depending on the J1N1 variant – between the pilot and observer or behind the observer. The J1N1-Sa, which could also be fitted with FD-2 AI radar in the nose, had three fuselage-mounted Type 99 weapons firing obliquely upward.

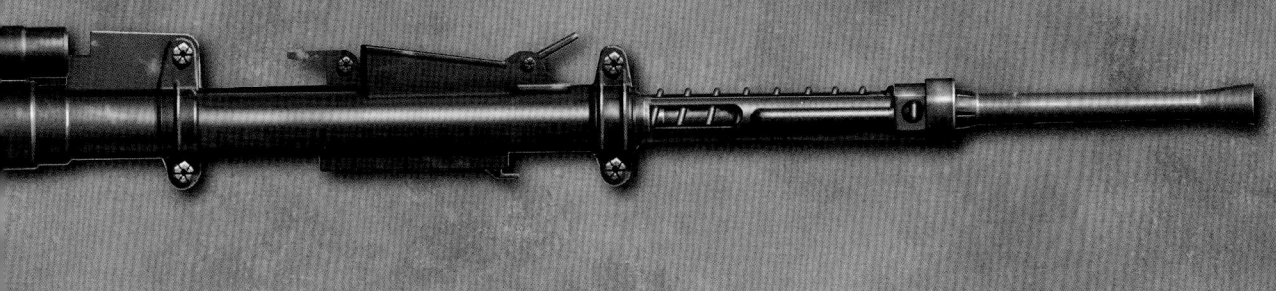

Japan was at the cutting edge of what became radar technology in the 1920s thanks to the pioneering work done by electrical engineer Hidetsugu Yagi in Osaka. As early as 1926, he patented the Yagi-Uda directional antenna (designed by his assistant Shintaro Uda) used by many radar receivers. Despite such developments, neither the IJAAF or the IJNAF were interested in fielding radio detection systems, and Japan fell behind the US, Great Britain, and Germany in the 1930s. The nation did not seriously pursue radar development until the early 1940s, just prior to the outbreak of the Pacific War.

Land-based Japanese radar became operational in the spring of 1942, with the first airborne radar following suit in August of that year in the form of the IJNAF's H-6, intended for surface searches. The IJAAF's first airborne radar, the Taki Mark 1, Type II finally appeared in mid-1943. At 330lb, it was too heavy for any aircraft except the IJAAF's largest bombers. A lightweight (176lb) Taki Mark 1, Type II subsequently appeared, and like its heavier precursor, it too operated on two-meter wavelengths.

Japan did not begin developing AI radar until December 1943, with the IJNAF and IJAAF pursuing independent development of nightfighter radars. The latter was unable to develop a functioning unit due to technical and production problems, resulting in its nightfighters lacking AI radar through to war's end. Just a solitary Ki-45 KAIc was tested with a centimetric radar mounted beneath a Plexiglas nose cover.

The IJNAF was more successful, developing three different nightfighter radars – the FD-1, FD-2, and TAMA3. Development of the FD-1 had started in December 1943, only to then be halted two months later. It was a prototype unit with a 60cm wavelength, a peak power of 2.5 kilowatts and the ability to spot individual aircraft 1.86 miles away. After work on the FD-1 ceased, development of the FD-2 began in April 1944. Using a 62cm wavelength, it was otherwise identical to the FD-1. Development concluded in August 1944, and it began to be installed in J1N1-Ss from

The Gekko was the sole Japanese nightfigher to carry AI radar operationally during World War II, and then only experimental, pre-production prototypes of the FD-2 set. The three Yagi antennas used by the radar were installed in the nose, replacing any forward-firing 20mm cannon previously mounted there. Many pilots preferred flying without radar equipment as a weight-saving measure. This particular aircraft is the world's sole surviving J1N1, which was shipped to the United States in 1946 for evaluation. (Tony Holmes Collection)

January 1945. Work on the TAMA3 commenced in September 1944, with the first units being delivered to operational units in July 1945. Using a two-meter wavelength, it was also capable of detecting targets 1.86 miles away. The TAMA3 arrived too late for use in combat, having failed to complete operational testing by the time the war ended.

Crews found the FD-2 difficult to use, and it never became widely operational despite 100 sets being delivered before war's end. Some pilots trialed the equipment in their Gekkos, while others decided the AI radar's 154lb weight, and associated external antenna attached to the aircraft's nose, reduced performance too much to justify using it. Regardless, this seems to have been the only AI radar fielded by the Japanese. Its use, even experimentally, might explain why most of the nation's nightfighter aces were IJNAF pilots.

The lack of reliable AI radar is a major reason for the ineffectiveness of Japanese nightfighters. Despite the FD-2 having a detection range of less than two miles, it could locate B-29s in a dark night sky far beyond a pilot's visual sighting range.

THE STRATEGIC SITUATION

Strategic bombing offered a means of avoiding static and ghastly trench warfare. Aircraft could bypass surface forces, flying over them to attack the enemy's rear. Air superiority meant bombers could pound anything within reach to rubble. And "the bomber will always get through," claimed former Prime Minister Stanley Baldwin, then Lord President of the Council of Great Britain (and soon to be Prime Minister for a third time), in a speech to the British Parliament on November 10, 1932.

Air power achieved its voice in the writings of Gen Giulio Douhet, an early advocate who served in the Italian Army from 1882. Since the start of the 20th century, he had been an advocate of military mechanization. The arrival of the aircraft shifted his focus to its potential, Douhet writing a manual on its military use in 1912. Expanding his vision during World War I, he distilled his beliefs into the book *Il dominio dell'aria* (*Command of the Air*) in 1921. It declared that command of the air meant victory. Translated into multiple languages, the book became a bible for air power advocates around the world during the interwar years.

Not every nation adopted all aspects of Douhet's vision, however. Germany, Japan, and Italy developed air forces to support their armies (and, for Japan, its navy, too). This went beyond using aircraft as flying artillery. Rather, they were used for deep strikes into the enemy's rear, destroying logistics and disrupting communications. European powers like France and the USSR lacked either the economic strength or the industrial base to produce the large quantities of heavy bombers required for a successful strategic campaign.

The United States and especially Britain became proponents of strategic bombing in the 1930s. For the RAF, the strategic bomber was the *only* bomber. Strategic bombardment was key to its operational future, the RAF selling the bomber to the government as the principle way to avoid a repeat of World War I's trench warfare. All such aircraft, from the single-engined Fairey Battle to the four-engined Short Stirling, were intended to be used as strategic bombers.

The USAAC, anchored to the US Army, was less invested in strategic bombing than the RAF. While not as absolutist as their British counterparts, USAAC advocates of strategic bombers were as enthusiastic about their potential in any future conflict.

By 1944 no nation had achieved victory through strategic air power. The Luftwaffe's attempts to prevail during the Battle of Britain in 1940 and the Blitz of 1940–41 had failed. RAF Bomber Command, despite 1,000-bomber raids and firestorm-generating incendiary missions, had also failed to force Germany to surrender through strategic bombardment, even with cooperative USAAF daylight heavy bomber raids. The bomber did not always get through. Duhout's predictions that civilian morale would collapse following sustained strategic bombing, forcing the government to surrender, failed to occur. Rather, aerial bombardment seemed to stiffen the resolve of the enemy population to fight on.

While it hurt the Germans, strategic bombing failed to end the war. That required boots on the ground, soldiers on enemy soil. Although air superiority had been the key to Allied success in Europe, the RAF and the USAAF needed the army and navy to secure victory. Air power advocates found that unsatisfactory. They wanted to demonstrate that aircraft alone could win a war. Indeed, the USAAF remained convinced that strategic air power, properly used, could still win a war unaided. It still believed precision bombardment – highly accurate targeting placing bombs on high-value enemy targets – was the solution, despite its failure in Europe. The USAAF believed it failed there because it lacked the right tools. A precision bombsight and large, long-range four-engined bombers were subsequently developed to fit the strategy.

In 1940, the USAAC had requested development of a new bomber – a next generation very heavy "super bomber" which could fly transcontinental distances at unprecedented altitudes and speeds, carrying a bomb load far greater than what could be flown by existing heavy bombers. Two aircraft were developed, the B-29 Superfortress and the B-32 Dominator. Both had a combat range of 3,200 miles and could cruise at 230mph, carry in excess of 20,000lb of bombs internally and were powered by four 2,200hp 18-cylinder radial engines.

The B-32 was evolutionary, being a larger, faster version of the B-24 heavy bomber that was intended to operate at between 10,000–20,000ft. The B-29 was revolutionary. The aircraft operated at 30,000ft, and its pressurized crew compartment allowed the crew to fly in shirtsleeve conditions. The bomber had four remotely controlled turrets, with computerized targeting. Only the tail guns were manned. The aircraft had a cylindrical cross section and an ovoid nose, with no break for the windscreen. Boeing named it the Superfortress.

By 1944 the new bomber was becoming operational, rolling off assembly lines, ready to be committed to combat. The USAAF believed the B-29 was the perfect aircraft to demonstrate the potential of strategic bombing. It also believed there was one last opportunity to demonstrate that potential against the perfect opponent for that purpose, the Empire of Japan.

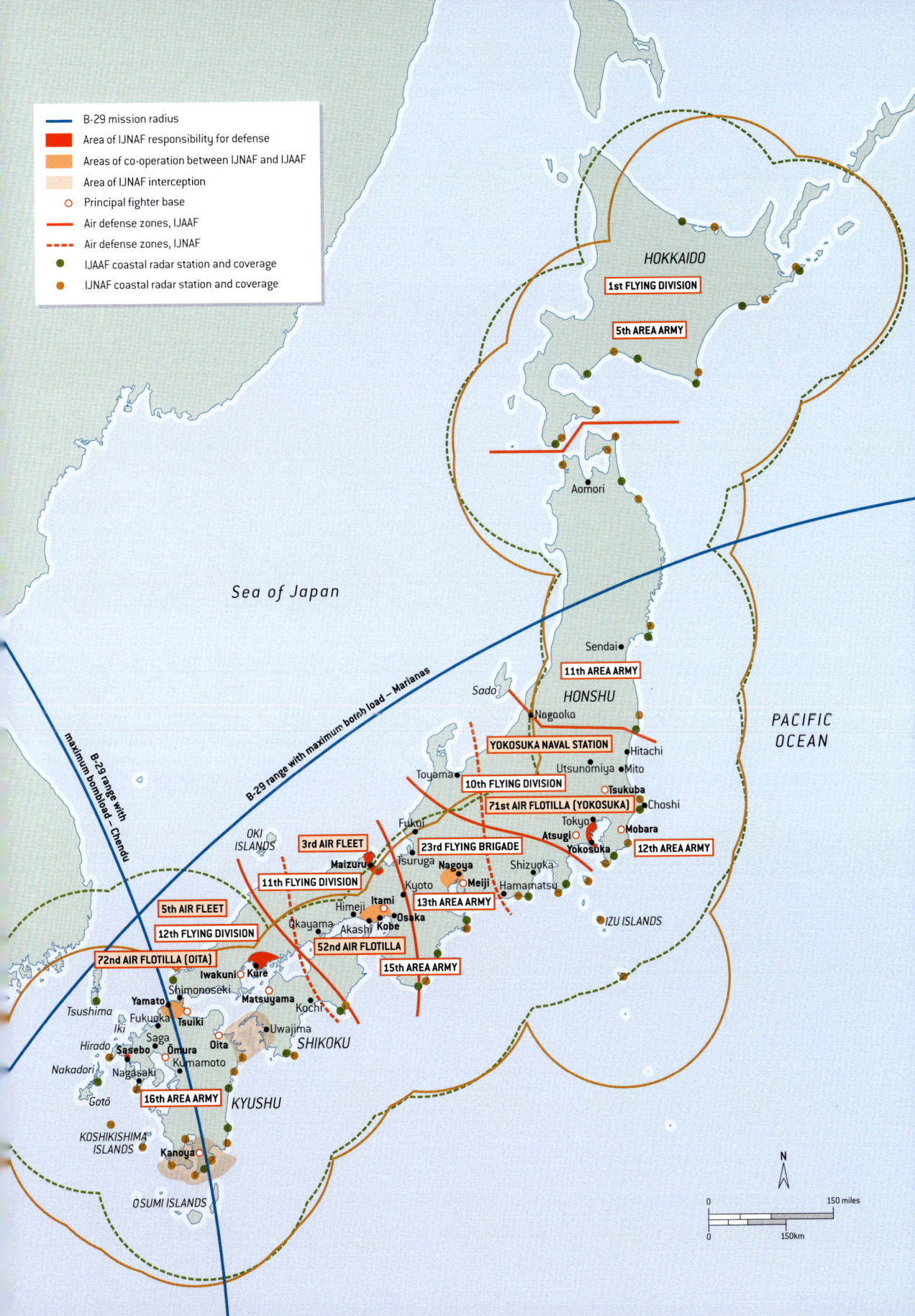

Legend:

- — B-29 mission radius
- ▮ Area of IJNAF responsibility for defense
- ▮ Areas of co-operation between IJNAF and IJAAF
- ▯ Area of IJNAF interception
- ○ Principal fighter base
- — Air defense zones, IJAAF
- – – Air defense zones, IJNAF
- ● IJAAF coastal radar station and coverage
- ● IJNAF coastal radar station and coverage

HOKKAIDO

1st FLYING DIVISION

5th AREA ARMY

Aomori

Sea of Japan

PACIFIC OCEAN

Sendai

11th AREA ARMY

HONSHU

Sado

Nagaoka

YOKOSUKA NAVAL STATION

Hitachi

Toyama

Utsunomiya Mito

10th FLYING DIVISION

Tsukuba

71st AIR FLOTILLA (YOKOSUKA)

Choshi

B-29 range with maximum bomb load – Marianas

Fukui

Tokyo

Mobara

OKI ISLANDS

3rd AIR FLEET

Maizuru

Tsuruga

Nagoya

Shizuoka

Atsugi

12th AREA ARMY

23rd FLYING BRIGADE

Yokosuka

11th FLYING DIVISION

Kyoto

Meiji

Hamamatsu

5th AIR FLEET

Itami

13th AREA ARMY

Himeji

Osaka

IZU ISLANDS

B-29 range with maximum bombload – Chengtu

12th FLYING DIVISION

Okayama

Akashi

Kobe

52nd AIR FLOTILLA

72nd AIR FLOTILLA (OITA)

Iwakuni

Kure

15th AREA ARMY

Tsushima

Yamato

Shimonoseki

Matsuyama

Kochi

Iki

Fukuoka

Tsuiki

Uwajima

SHIKOKU

Hirado

Saga

Oita

Nakadori

Sasebo

Ōmura

Kumamoto

Nagasaki

Gotō

16th AREA ARMY

KYUSHU

KOSHIKISHIMA ISLANDS

Kanoya

OSUMI ISLANDS

N

0   150 miles

0   150km

Japan and the United States had been moving towards war with each other throughout the 1930s. In 1931 Japan invaded Manchuria. After a six-month war with China it annexed Manchuria, creating the Republic of Manchukuo. In 1937 Japan attacked China, starting the Second Sino-Japanese War. When the campaign got mired down, Japanese troops began capturing Chinese ports in order to isolate China. In September 1940, Japan commenced the occupation of French Indochina.

Japanese aggression alarmed the United States, which began implementing economic sanctions. Japan had occupied all of French Indochina in July 1941, after which it began threatening the US protectorate of the Philippines. The United States countered with an oil embargo on Japan, convincing Great Britain and the Netherlands to do the same. This left Japan with only a six-month reserve of oil before its military ground to a halt. The nation's Supreme War Council duly decided to seize the resources Japan needed in the region from the Western powers, attacking territory overseen by the United States (the Philippines and Hawaii), the British Empire (Malaya and Singapore), and the Netherlands (Dutch East Indies) in December 1941.

For six months the IJA and IJN advanced virtually unchecked, establishing a perimeter that ran from the Indian border in the east, through the Dutch East Indies, British/Australian-held territory in the South Pacific, the coral atolls of the Marshall and Gilbert Islands, Wake Island, and the Aleutian chain.

Over the next two years the Allies pushed Japan back, capturing the Marianas in June–July 1944. It marked the beginning of the end for Japan, and its government began seeking a way to sue for peace rather than being militarily defeated. The Allies would be satisfied by nothing less than unconditional surrender. By the end of 1944 the Philippines was in the process of being recaptured and plans were in place to capture the Bonin and Ryukyu Islands preparatory to invading the Japanese Home Islands. Projected casualties were half-a-million to a million Allied soldiers and five to ten million Japanese dead.

By June 1944 the B-29 was operational. It had the range to attack Japan from airfields in China and the Marianas, thus offering air power advocates one final chance to demonstrate the potential of strategic bombing. Allied war leaders were willing to give the USAAF that chance before launching a ground invasion of the Home Islands. If the enemy could be brought to its knees by bombing, invasion would be unnecessary.

Japan seemed to be the perfect "laboratory" to demonstrate the decisive nature of strategic bombardment. While a major industrial nation, it was the smallest of the industrial powers, bar Italy. Being an island nation, Japan could be isolated by a sea blockade and naval mines. It had adequate domestic sources of iron and coal, but virtually everything else had to be imported. The

Maj Gen Curtis E. LeMay (right), then CO of XX Bomber Command, greets Gen Joseph Stillwell, deputy supreme Allied commander of South East Asia Command, at Hsinching airfield, in China, on October 11, 1944. LeMay singlehandedly reversed the fortunes of the B-29 in the strategic bombing campaign against the Home Islands. (Library of Congress (LOC))

USAAF believed it could destroy Japan's war industries, stop its communications and neutralize its military bases through strategic bombing with the B-29.

The USAAF established XX Bomber Command in November 1943 and placed all operational B-29s under its control, sending early examples of the aircraft to attack Japan from newly constructed bases in India and China as part of Operation *Matterhorn*. The first B-29 strike against the Home Islands occurred on June 15, 1944, launched from China. Subsequent operations by XX Bomber Command were restricted by the excessive range to targets in Japan, logistical supply problems to Chinese airfields and the vulnerability of the latter to attacks by the enemy. Poor serviceability of early B-29s also had an adverse effect on XX Bomber Command.

Following the May 24–25, 1945 fire raid on Tokyo, the city's commercial district was left in total ruins. Although this photograph was taken immediately postwar during the Allied occupation of Japan, it starkly captures the result of the attack, which burned out both this part of the capital and the adjacent government district. Nighttime area incendiary raids transformed the B-29 from an ineffective technical marvel into a deadly effective war-winning weapon. Unchecked, the raids burned out the industrial heart of Japan, reducing the nation's production of war materials to levels that left it incapable of supporting its military forces. (LOC)

Following the first B-29 strike on Tokyo from the Marianas by XXI Bomber Command in November 1944, the focus of all strategic bombing operations quickly shifted away from China to the Pacific islands. As had been the case with XX Bomber Command, early missions by XXI Bomber Command proved to be as ineffective as the European strategic bombing campaign. The cost of the raids to the Allies in aircrew and aircraft was acceptable, but damage being done by the bombers was trivial. Unless XXI Bomber Command delivered decisive results the strategic bombardment campaign would be abandoned.

In January 1945 XXI Bomber Command received a new commanding officer in the form of Maj Gen Curtis E. LeMay, formerly CO of XX Bomber Command. A fixer, he had made his reputation solving problems and meeting goals. In this case, his goal was to make the B-29 effective. LeMay chose to supplement precision attacks with area bombing. He also supported using B-29s to drop naval mines in Japanese waters, viewing this as an extension of strategic bombing. Both were anathema to the precision bombing purists in the USAAF. LeMay cared less about doctrinal purity than achieving results.

On March 9, 1945 he launched a massive fire raid against Tokyo. The results achieved in this single attack dwarfed the damage done to Japan in all the previous air raids against the Home Islands from the April 1942 Doolittle Raid until the first Tokyo fire raid. LeMay followed this attack up with subsequent area raids that proved equally devastating. On March 27 XXI Bomber Command launched Operation *Starvation*, the campaign to isolate Japan by sea through mining. The two types of missions were very different. The fire raids were mass attacks, using as many aircraft as was available – including 560 in one mission – to inflict widespread destruction. Minelaying missions involved just 24 to 48 B-29s dropping mines with a high degree of precision. They shared two characteristics, though. They were both war-winning attacks flown at night.

THE COMBATANTS

The battle between B-29s and Japanese nightfighters pitted two groups of highly motivated men against each other. Both were selected as aircrew from the best candidates each country had. They were physically fit, had perfect eyesight, and superior reflexes. They were also intelligent and educated. All were volunteers, and they had qualified for their positions following rigorous training. Both sets of men wanted to win.

There were important differences between the men of the opposing forces, however. By late 1944, when their confrontation with Japanese nightfighters began in earnest, USAAF aircrew were better trained than their IJAAF and IJNAF counterparts. The Japanese air forces had been hollowed out by combat casualties and inadequate replacement policies. The USAAF had applied mass-production techniques to its aircrew training without adversely affecting the quality of graduates, allowing it to produce better trained personnel in much greater numbers.

Additionally, the USAAF sent its most experienced personnel into the B-29 program. When the campaign started, XXI Bomber Command had a core of combat veterans who had extensively trained on the new platform prior to manning its aircraft. Conversely, the IJAAF and IJNAF staffed their nightfighters with whoever was available. Although some were experienced, many, despite the challenging nature of night flying, were not.

B-29 CREWMAN

The Superfortress crew numbered ten or eleven men. Each B-29 had an aircraft commander, co-pilot, bombardier, navigator, flight engineer, radio operator and four aerial gunners. Bombers equipped with ECM carried an electronics officer called a

"Raven." Flying the B-29 was complicated enough to require a third pilot, called the flight engineer, to monitor and control the engines and other mechanical aspects of the bomber while the aircraft commander and co-pilot flew the Superfortress. The B-29 was so advanced the USAAF changed crew titles to reflect the additional skill flying these aircraft required.

Although the gunners were enlisted men, most of the remaining crew were commissioned officers – another indication of the advanced nature of the B-29. On other four-engined bombers the radio operator and flight engineer were typically enlisted ranks operating less complicated systems. All were volunteers, having been selected for flight status because of their intelligence, physical excellence, and mechanical aptitude. They were among the best men the USAAF had, having been handpicked, especially when the B-29 program began. Most were combat veterans chosen from personnel that had flown four-engined aircraft operationally. Amongst their ranks were men who had completed tours in Europe.

The USAAF also used crews from its Antisubmarine Command who had flown maritime patrols in B-24s. In April 1943, following disagreements with the US Navy over the conduct of the antisubmarine warfare mission, the USAAF agreed to stop such operations and transfer all of the command's Liberators to the Second Air Force – the primary training organization for B-17 and B-24 heavy bombardment groups. Two wings were also disbanded in November of that year, freeing up personnel just as the B-29 began to enter service. It gave the USAAF a pool of aircrew experienced in conducting long flights over water, similar to the missions Superfortresses would subsequently fly. Many were transferred to the new program.

As the B-29 force grew in size, personnel straight out of training joined XX/XXI Bomber Command, and the percentage of those with prior combat experience dropped. Even so, aircrew destined to man B-29s were chosen from the top graduates of their training classes.

By late 1944, when the B-29 first began facing Japanese nightfighters, most USAAF personnel were wartime volunteers. On June 30, 1938, the USAAC had numbered only 20,196 personnel. This total had increased to nearly 2.4 million officers and enlisted personnel by late 1944, the USAAC having become the USAAF almost three years earlier. Despite rapid expansion, the USAAF maintained high standards for aircrew. Initially, applicants for aviation cadet training – which led to an officer's commission – had to be between 20 and 26 years old, and to have completed at least two years of college. Enlisted applicants were between 18 and 30 years old, with at least an eighth grade education. Volunteers were screened for aptitude and assigned to appropriate training.

In 1941 aircrew candidates could be no taller than 5ft 10in. and weigh no more than 170lb. They had to be physically fit, with 20/20 eyesight and good hearing. These

USAAF volunteers went through basic training, where they learned skills needed by soldiers – physical fitness, squad, platoon and company drill, marching, and ceremonies. Officer candidates did this in a college ROTC program, while enlisted men went through a Basic Training Center. Here, AT-17 Bobcat trainers fly in close formation overhead while officer candidates march at Ellington Field near Houston, Texas. (Author's Collection)

41

qualifications for admission were successively modified, with the age limit being raised to 35 years, height to six feet and weight to 180lb. Although education, vision and eyesight requirements remained fixed, there were waivers for candidates with prior aviation experience, especially early in the war.

Upon entry to the USAAF, enlistees went through basic training. Officer candidates did this in a college program with the Reserve Officer Training Corps (ROTC), which included pre-flight ground schools. Enlisted personnel attended a Basic Training Center, where, from 1940 through to 1943, they completed four weeks of training that saw them accrue 192 hours of instruction. For much of this time recruits undertook the "School of the Soldier" – physical training, squad drill, platoon drill, company drill, marching, and ceremonies. No marksmanship or small arms training was given.

The Basic Training Center syllabus increased in length to eight weeks from mid-1943 to accommodate ground combat skills. Following the completion of the Basic Training Center course, enlisted men were sent to technical schools for specialized tuition, including fight training. All B-29 aircrew were specialists, which meant that they received specialized training in their field of expertise.

When pilot candidates went through flight training, there were three stages to complete – primary, basic, and advanced. Primary training taught students to fly a low-horsepower small aircraft. Much of this took place in civilian schools. For trainees in an education program, this was done during college. Basic flight training put would-be aviators in heavier, more complex aircraft. Advanced training had them fly aircraft with characteristics of frontline types. Bomber pilot training was done on multi-engined trainers like the Curtiss-Wright AT-9 Jeep, Beechcraft AT-10 Wichita, and Cessna AT-17 Bobcat. Students received their wings and were commissioned as second lieutenants upon completing advanced training. It typically took 70–75 flight hours to earn pilot's wings. New pilots next undertook specialized instruction suited to their military assignments, and this included the final stage of individual training whereby aviators transitioned to the aircraft they would fly in combat. At this point pilots started training as members of both a crew and a combat unit.

A school for B-29 flight engineers was created in April 1943. Its syllabus consisted of a 19-week training course run by enlisted instructors, but whose graduates received commissions. It was divided into basic and advanced courses, with graduates going to a B-29 transition school. Initially, modified B-24s were used for flight training.

USAAC navigation schools had been established in November 1940, with candidates undertaking a 15-week course that trained them in dead reckoning, celestial navigation, pilotage (navigating by compass heading), radio navigation,

Pilots who ended up flying heavy bombers, including B-29s, learned to fly multi-engined aircraft as part of their advanced flight training. Typically, this was done using AT-9 Jeeps (seen here), AT-10 Wichitas, and AT-17 Bobcats. These were general aviation aircraft modified into trainers. (Author's Collection)

and eventually radar navigation. This involved 500 hours of ground school and 100 hours of flight instruction.

Specialized bombardier training began in July 1941. Through to mid-1943, it was a 12-week course, which was lengthened to 18 weeks thereafter. There was a shortage of qualified bombardiers, which meant B-17 and B-24 squadrons often had to train enlisted aircrew to undertake the role after they joined their units, tutoring them in-house. All bombardiers sent to B-29 units were graduates of the formal bombardier school, however. This meant that they had completed the ten-week "Bombing Through Overcast" (radar-bombing) course added to the bombardier training curriculum in 1944.

Radio operators undertook a six-month course that involved 720 hours of instruction on the use and operation of aircraft radios. In October 1943, the first five-week radar observer course commenced, and it was open to graduates of the radio operator course. Graduates of the standard officer communications course were also selected for a 15-week radar course. "Ravens" were drawn from men who had completed the latter.

Navigators, bombardiers, and enlisted aircrew went through a six-week aerial gunnery course. Some enlisted aircrew had no other speciality – they were "career gunners." Such individuals were given priority for gunnery schools, which experienced a shortage of recruits through to June 1944. They provided training on maintaining and operation of the 0.50-cal. machine gun, ground/aerial firing training, and specialized training on specific power turrets.

Because of the revolutionary nature of the B-29, the USAAF created a familiarization school for all aircrew flying the Superfortress. Aircraft commanders, pilots, and flight engineers trained together as a team in a five-week course. Bombardiers, navigators, and radio operators went through very long range training (in preparation for operations in the Pacific) in their specialties after completing standard courses. The bombardier and all four gunners needed a specialized gunnery school to train them in how to use the B-29's Central Station Fire Control System.

Following the completion of training for their primary positions, personnel received instruction to allow them to undertake other roles within the B-29. While expected to be an expert in how their own system functioned operationally, aircrew also benefited from significant cross-training. Gunners had to understand how to operate all four turrets effectively, and bombardiers, navigators, and radio operators had to be capable of undertaking all three roles, as well as fulfilling the role of flight engineer if necessary. Crews also went through a period of integrated training, for not only did the aircraft commander, pilot, and flight engineer routinely work together, the navigator and radio operator coordinated closely during different portions of the mission.

The commander, pilot, and flight engineer of the B-29 trained as a team. In many ways, the B-29's flight engineer was essentially a third pilot, controlling the throttles, monitoring the engines and managing the aircraft's fuel during a mission. Early B-29s had some enlisted flight engineers, including MSgt Harry Miller, seen here at the engineer's instrument panel following a raid on Anshan, in Manchuria, during Operation *Matterhorn*. By 1945 most flight engineers were officers. (NMAF)

ROBERT K. MORGAN

Robert Knight Morgan was born on July 31, 1918 in Asheville, North Carolina. His father managed and later owned a furniture manufacturing company. Morgan was educated at Christ School, a private college preparatory school in Asheville, before attending Wharton School of Finance at the University of Pennsylvania prior to World War II. He also worked at Morgan Manufacturing, the family business, during that period and married and divorced for the first time.

Morgan joined the USAAC as a pilot cadet in December 1940, despite initially failing the eye exam. He passed with the aid of a sympathetic doctor who allowed Morgan to memorize the eye chart. He reported for primary flight training at Woodward Field in Camden, South Carolina, in May 1941, followed by basic training at Daniel Army Airfield in Augusta, Georgia, two months later. Upon completing basic training, Morgan was sent to Barksdale Field, Shreveport, Louisiana, in September for advanced flight training in heavy bombers. Following graduation, he was commissioned as a second lieutenant.

Between marrying again on December 26, 1941 and the spring of 1942, Morgan qualified as a command pilot for the Lockheed A-29 and the B-24, and was again divorced. In May he was reassigned to the 324th BS/91st BG equipped with B-17s. After intense training, the group was sent to England as part of the Eighth Air Force. Prior to departing for the European Theater of Operations, Morgan met Margaret Polk from Memphis, Tennessee, and got engaged, subsequently naming his B-17F for her – *Memphis Belle*. Morgan and *Memphis Belle* completed 25 missions over German-occupied Europe, including six over Germany itself. Only the second Flying Fortress to do so, *Memphis Belle* and its crew became the subject of a documentary as the first B-17 to complete a 25-mission tour. In June 1943 both the aircraft and its crew were sent back to the United States on a War Bond tour. By the end of the tour (and a stint providing dialog for the *Memphis Belle* documentary), Morgan had broken off his engagement to Polk.

In October 1943 Morgan transitioned to the B-29, joining the 497th BG the following month as the commander of its 869th BS. The unit deployed to the Pacific as part of the 73rd BW in September 1944. By then Morgan was married again, to Dorothy Johnson. He named his B-29 *Dauntless*

Capt Robert Knight Morgan, photographed stateside following the completion of his B-17 tour with the Eighth Air Force and prior to transferring to the B-29-equipped 869th BS as its CO. (Author's Collection)

Dotty in her honor. It was only the second Superfortress to land at Saipan. Morgan flew 26 combat missions during his Pacific tour, 12 of them to Tokyo – he led the first bombing mission mounted by B-29s against the Japanese capital on November 24, 1944. Morgan also flew two night missions: the first such raid on Tokyo on March 9, 1945 and the first incendiary raid on Osaka four days later. He was rotated home in April 1945.

Morgan left active duty after World War II had ended, although he remained in the USAF Reserve until 1965, retiring as a colonel. Postwar, he was an executive in the family furniture business and later owned a Volkswagen dealership in Virginia. After retirement, Morgan became active on the airshow circuit. He died on May 5, 2004 following a fall the previous month.

Training continued even after the crews' arrival in-theater. The first missions flown by most crews were "milk runs" – operations combing a long flight with a low-risk target. A typical example of these operations were those flown against targets on Truk Atoll, formerly the IJN's main naval base in the South Pacific some 600 miles from the Marianas. It had been effectively isolated from Japan following a series of strikes by US Navy carrier-based aircraft in Operation *Hailstone* in February 1944. Missions against Truk provided new B-29 crews with overwater experience, light enemy resistance and a valid target.

Teamwork would become a watchword for B-29 crews. They stuck together, attempting to stay with personnel familiar to them. The best illustration of this occurred during XXI Bomber Command's first night missions, when aircraft were to sortie with all their guns, bar those in the tail turret, without ammunition. Maj Gen LeMay wanted to leave the gunners behind, thus saving weight for extra bombs and fuel, but many of them protested at the prospect of being left on the ground. They wanted to keep their team together. To preserve moral, LeMay allowed the crews to fly intact.

JAPANESE FIGHTER PILOT

The Japanese pilots who flew against the B-29s, including those flying nightfighters, were neither as well trained nor as skilled as their opponents manning Superfortresses. Even in late 1944, when the first night raids were flown against Japan, they lacked the training levels of the then still "green" B-29 crews. By March 1945, when the main night offensive against Japan began, the typical nightfighter pilot had less experience and training than his mid-1944 counterpart.

At the beginning of the Pacific War in December 1941, Japan possessed a force of highly skilled pilots. Half were combat veterans of the Second Sino-Japanese War, being the "harvest" of two decades worth of training and preparation. The IJAAF and the IJNAF had established formal pilot training programs in 1920, which they then gradually expanded. By 1940 the IJAAF was graduating 750 and the IJNAF 2,000 pilots annually. Both services maintained strictly separate pools of aircrew personnel. On December 7, 1941, Japan had a total of 12,000 trained aircrew, 7,500 (3,500 of whom were pilots) in the IJNAF and 4,500 (2,500 pilots) in the IJAAF.

Officer pilots averaged 300 flying hours before being sent to combat units, as opposed to 200 flying hours for their US counterparts. Aviators, both IJAAF and IJNAF, who flew aircraft in Japan's opening offensives averaged 600 flying hours prior to reaching the frontline. Some 600 IJNAF pilots were assigned to carrier air groups. Those men, who had typically accrued 800 flying hours prior to being declared operational, went through rigorous training before joining fleet units.

Prewar, IJAAF officer pilot candidates attended an air academy for two years, during which time six months of flight training was provided. Successful air academy completion was followed by a further year of flight training at air schools. Those who passed were commissioned and sent to an operational flying regiment as the final stage of their flight training. The best officers were selected for leadership school, a three- to six-month program intended to prepare pilots for higher command.

IJNAF officer pilot training followed a different path. All regular pilot candidates were commissioned officer graduates of the IJN's Naval Academy at Etajima prior to them commencing flight training. Recruits initially spent two months at ground school before undertaking primary and basic flight training. The latter took six months to complete, during which time candidates accrued 60 flying hours in trainers. They then had to pass operational flight training, logging 100 hours at the controls of obsolete combat aircraft. Upon earning their wings, pilots were given tactical flight training by frontline units, requiring the accumulation of 150 flying hours before being deemed ready for operations.

The IJNAF also had a reserve officer pilot program open to college graduates who passed the physical. They went through four months of preflight training, with eight weeks being spent familiarizing officer candidates with military courtesy and naval tradition, rather like the USAAF and US Navy ROTC programs. Upon completion, they were fed into the primary, basic, and operational flight training programs used by regular IJN officers.

Japan, unlike the United States but like most other major powers, had enlisted pilots in both the IJAAF and the IJNAF. Pre-war, regular enlisted personnel attended boys' air preparatory schools prior to formally enlisting in the IJA. Having graduated from their "prep" schools, they went through a one-year basic flight training course. Once this was completed, they were made NCOs and sent to frontline units to complete their tuition.

IJNAF enlisted applicants for flight training were volunteers drawn from serving members of the IJN's surface forces. Once selected, they undertook six months of preflight training before moving to primary and basic flight training, which also took six months to complete. As with pilots on the officer course, they were allocated just 44 flying hours in training. The next stage was operational flight training, which saw aviators accumulate a further 60 hours aloft. During the final training phase, known as tactical flight training, pilots tallied 150 flying hours each.

Once war began, existing training programs proved inadequate. Too few pilots were available and aircrew wastage was high, for the IJAAF and IJNAF devoted minimal effort to recovering downed aviators. If they could not get to friendly lines unaided, they were generally lost.

The IJAAF had recognized the need for more pilots prior to the start of hostilities in the Pacific. It implemented prewar plans to expand pilot training in December 1941, and by early the following year 18 new units had formed to train reserve personnel. Reserve officer candidates required two years at either a technical school or college. Enlisted personnel with these qualifications

The majority of the IJNAF's pilots were enlisted men. This group of extremely youthful trainee aviators are posing with a K5Y1 Type 93 Intermediate Trainer. (Tony Holmes Collection)

could also apply, offering them a path to a commission, while reserve enlisted candidates had to have graduated from a secondary school.

Once accepted into an air school, all reserve recruits went through compressed flight training that took a year to complete, while regular officers and enlisted personnel followed a compressed version of the prewar training course that was completed in eight to ten months.

1Lt Tsuru of 53rd Sentai instructs pilots on the correct approach tactics for attacking a B-29 at night in front of one of the unit's Ki-45 KAIcs at Matsudo, less than 15 miles northeast of central Tokyo. Seated seventh from the left is Sgt Nobuji Negishi, who would end the war as the Sentai's leading B-29 killer with six destroyed and seven damaged. The unit claimed an astonishing 168 B-29s destroyed or damaged between November 1944 and July 1945. (Tony Holmes Collection)

After this, they were assigned to operational units for final flight training. The reserve training program allowed the IJAAF to produce 4,200 pilots in both 1942 and 1943 – a significant increase from the prewar 750.

The IJNAF did not begin increasing its training until late 1942, when it formed two dedicated air groups. It created two more in early 1943. Flight training was compressed following the commencement of hostilities, with preflight training being dropped in early 1942. The IJNAF produced 2,300 pilots in 1942 and 2,700 in 1943. These numbers were inadequate, for the two services lost a combined total of 10,000 pilots in 1942–43 – more than were trained during that same period. The majority of those killed were experienced aviators, since Japan did not relieve or rotate pilots out of the frontline. They flew until they either perished or were so badly wounded they had to return to the Home Islands to recover.

By December 1943, the average flying hours amongst the surviving pilots had fallen from 700 to 500 for the IJNAF and from 500 to 250 for the IJAAF. This meant that the average flying hours of *all* IJAAF pilots was only 50 hours greater than for USAAF pilots joining operational units straight out of flight school.

Both services again increased their training efforts from late 1943, with the IJNAF having tripled the number of air groups allocated to pilot instruction by mid-1944. The IJAAF also vastly expanded its training units, locating many of the new schools in the Philippines for better proximity to refineries in the Dutch East Indies. Fuel shortages in the Home Islands were becoming commonplace by late 1943 due to the loss of tankers to US Navy submarines. Borneo to Manila was a shorter, less hazardous tanker voyage than Borneo to Formosa or Kyushu, requiring fewer such vessels to be used. The combined goal for both services was to train 30,000 pilots in 1944.

A lack of fuel meant that training had to be further compressed for both services. The IJAAF not only reduced enlisted flight training to as little as six months, it lowered admission standards. Before the war, all candidates admitted had to be outstanding physical specimens. Many of those chosen for flight training in 1944 would have been disqualified just three years earlier. Additionally, flying hours for training plummeted, especially after September 1944 when fuel restrictions began to really bite and Allied air forces started attacking training bases, particularly those in the Philippines.

By June 1944, when the first B-29 raid against Japan was flown, average flying hours for IJNAF and IJAAF pilots were 375 and 175 hours, respectively.

Japan's best nightfighters were twin-engined aircraft significantly more complicated than the single-engined fighters IJAAF and IJNAF pilots typically flew. Most senior aviators – the ones with the most experience – preferred to fly the latest generation single-engined fighters, not twin-engined aircraft with designs predating the Pacific War. Only a few surviving "old hands" who had flown Ki-45s since they had become operational in 1942 preferred sticking with them.

Capt Koji Kobayashi, the Hikotai leader of 4th Sentai, salutes his pilots at Ozuki, in Western Honshu, in 1944–45. Behind them are ten Ki-45 KAIs, which the Sentai flew from early 1943 through to war's end. Despite such shows of strength, IJAAF nightfighter Sentai were largely ineffective. Too many of their pilots lacked the multi-engined or night-flying hours necessary to use their Ki-45s effectively. Nevertheless, during four night engagements between June 1944 and July 1945, 4th Sentai crews were credited with destroying 31 B-29s, probably destroying 14 more and damaging a further 14. (Tony Holmes Collection)

The Home Islands were a backwater in 1944, which meant that experienced nightfighter pilots were to be found in more active theaters such as the Philippines or Burma. Aviators with less experience were assigned to the Home Islands, largely to build up more flying time. By March 1945, when the US night bombing campaign began in earnest, the aviators charged with Japan's defense were the most experienced nightfighter pilots remaining in the IJAAF and IJNAF. Many of their comrades had been killed defending the Philippines, Burma or the Dutch East Indies.

Pilots who completed training between June 1944 and January 1945 (when most conventional flight schools ceased operating) were even less prepared. They were being transferred into frontline squadrons after completing as little as 100 flying hours. The Home Islands' nightfighter force had been gutted between November 1944 and February 1945 during ineffective daylight attacks against formations of B-29s. Except for the lucky few experienced survivors, Japan's nocturnal air defense was in the hands of pilots often lacking the skills required to safely land their aircraft at night, much less find and intercept an enemy B-29.

This J1N1-S was assigned to 210th Kokutai, formed at Meiji, in Aichi Prefecture, in September 1944. The unit trained fighter, bomber, dive-bomber and torpedo-bomber pilots, and also undertook B-29 interception missions in the defense of Nagoya from mid-December. (Tony Holmes Collection)

YASUNA KOZONO

Yasuna Kozono was the "father" of the IJNAF's nightfighter force, being a long-serving pilot in the IJNAF. Born on November 1, 1902 in Minamisatsuma in Kagoshima Prefecture on Kyushu, Kozono entered the IJN's Naval Academy in August 1920 following his graduation from Tachikawa Junior High School. Three years later, he was commissioned as an ensign in the IJN. Kozono eventually became an IJNAF pilot, being assigned to the carrier *Ryujo* after achieving his flightdeck qualification in the early 1930s. In October 1935, Kozono, then a lieutenant, was given command of the *Ryujo* air group, becoming the carrier's senior aviator. Fourteen months later, in December 1936, he was promoted to lieutenant commander. Kozono saw combat in the opening year of the Second Sino-Japanese War, taking part in attacks on Hangzhou, Guangde, and Nanjing in August–September 1937. In December, Kozono's air group commenced operations from Guangde airfield on the Chinese mainland.

Lt Cdr Yasuna Kozono (center) with his staff possibly at Kunda, in China, in 1938 during the Second Sino-Japanese War (Author's Collection)

By 1942, having attained the rank of commander, Kozono was air executive officer of the Zero-sen-equipped Tainan Kokutai in the South Pacific theater. Redesignated 251st Kokutai on November 1, 1942, the unit was transferred back to Japan for a refit shortly thereafter. While in Japan, Kozono argued for arming 251st Kokutai's J1N1-C reconnaissance aircraft with obliquely firing guns as nightfighters following a series of increasingly effective nocturnal bombing raids on Rabaul by B-17s and B-24s during the summer/fall of 1942. Although the proposal was officially rejected, Kozono persisted, and a combination of his bullying, cooperative technical personnel, and subsequent practical success resulted in the conversion of J1N1 airframes held by the Yokosuka Air Arsenal into nightfighters.

Kozono had been given command of 251st Kokutai by the time the unit returned to Rabaul in May 1943. After arrival, the nightfighter J1N1 conversions proved successful, with a handful of B-17s and a B-24 being downed in a ten-day period. Kozono's innovation was subsequently adopted by both the IJNAF and the IJAAF, with J1N1-C/Ss and Ki-45s being fitted with obliquely firing guns for use as nightfighters.

In September 1943 Kozono was posted back to Japan, where he was promoted to captain and given command of

Atsugi airfield, arguably the IJNAF's most important base in the Home Islands, 31 miles southwest of Tokyo. From here, he would play a significant role in the IJNAF's air defense of the capital in 1944–45, directing the activities of 302nd Kokutai (which he also commanded) from March 1944 through to war's end.

Following Emperor Hirohito's announcement of Japan's surrender on August 15, 1945, Kozono led a group of die-hards refusing to surrender, dropping leaflets urging continuation of the war. The leaflets argued the Emperor's broadcast did not reflect his true position, but had been forced upon him by "traitors to the throne." The insurrectionists refused to obey orders from their superiors to surrender. Despite pleas from Prince Takamatsu, the Emperor's brother and a captain in the IJN, Kozono and 33 followers flew to IJAAF airfields in adjacent Saitama Prefecture on August 21 in an attempt to rally support for their cause. However, when this failed, they surrendered to Japanese authorities four days later. Arrested by the IJN and court martialed for insubordination, Kozono was sentenced to life imprisonment and stripped of his pension. The sentence was later reduced, and he was released from prison in December 1950 under parole for the rest of his sentence. Amnestied in 1952, Kozono became a farmer, dying of a cerebral hemorrhage on November 1, 1958.

COMBAT

Nightfighting presented more challenges than any other form of aerial combat. Restricted vision greatly affected the pilot's ability to locate landmarks or opposing aircraft. Simply flying straight and level at night was difficult due to the loss of visual cues. Flying exclusively by data provided by the aircraft's instrument panel required more training than visual flying. It also split a pilot's attention. He needed to simultaneously scan an instrument panel three feet from his eyes while watching the sky outside his aircraft for distant objects. For bomber pilots, distant objects on the ground were their targets. For nightfighter pilots, distant objects in the air were their targets – enemy bombers. Technology could reduce but not eliminate these difficulties. Radar gave better acquisition range, but required more time looking inside the cockpit.

Light was simultaneously a friend and an enemy. Humans required light to see. Any light on an enemy aircraft, or light contrast between an aircraft and its background, allowed detection. That was good. Any light produced by your aircraft allowed it to be detected. That was bad.

A B-29 of the 314th BW returns to Guam at the completion of a night mission. This unit was one of three wings that participated in the first Tokyo fire raid on March 9–10, 1945. To ensure that he had the maximum number of Superfortresses possible to perform this operation, Maj Gen LeMay ordered XXI Bomber Command to observe a five-day mission stand down immediately prior to the Tokyo attack. (NMAF)

Nocturnal air combat required rules that were completely different to those observed during air combat in daylight hours. Bombing missions were conducted in ways completely different to the methods used in daytime raids. Similarly, nightfighters fought using different rules to day fighters. Both found ways to ease handicaps imposed by darkness, while best using the advantages darkness offered. Yet bombers and fighters shared one common feature – they acted alone. There were no bomber or fighter formations. It was a one-on-one battle, with the crews of both aircraft working to outwit and outfight each other.

Understanding how the battles between B-29s and the nightfighters stalking them worked requires knowledge of three things:

1. How a night raid was conducted. What the objectives of a night raid were, how those objectives were achieved and why it was conducted in the manner used by XXI Bomber Command.
2. How nightfighters operated. How they found their quarry, the methods used to attack a target and the limitations faced by nightfighters.
3. How B-29 crews defended themselves against attacks by nightfighters. What actions could they take to detect and deter a pursuing nightfighter, and what steps could they use if attacked.

THE NIGHT RAID

While many night raids were area fire bombing missions, others attempted nighttime precision bombardment, including those flown against Japan from China. Regardless, night missions had a unique profile that meant they had to be countered in a manner completely different from the methods used to oppose B-29s undertaking daytime raids. The latter were flown with the bombers in a tight formation at high altitudes (typically in excess of 30,000ft, but later as low as 24,000ft). Night missions were flown at moderate altitudes (above 5,000ft but below 18,000ft), without formation flying.

At night, aircraft took off individually, flying to the target without forming up on other bombers. B-29s were given a course and an altitude range to follow. In multi-wing missions, each wing was given a different path and altitude range over the target so as to minimize the chance of collision. This had several positive effects. A night mission required significantly less fuel, resulting in a weight saving that could be transferred to the bombload. Aircraft did not waste fuel forming up before heading to the target. They also did not use fuel reaching an altitude of 30,000ft. Further bombload weight was gained by leaving the top turret machine guns unloaded in the first 1945 night raids, and only carrying ammunition for the tail guns on later missions. The first Tokyo night raid saw bombers loaded with 12,000lb of incendiaries rather than the 4,000–5,000lb of bombs carried on previous daytime strikes. Finally, night missions did not require crews to face frigid temperatures or low pressure flying at high altitude, thus reducing fatigue.

Initially, crews saw night missions rather differently, however. They believed that they were going into the heart of Japan alone and without support at suicidality low

1. Airspeed indicator
2. Altimeter
3. Turn-and-bank indicator
4. Rate-of-climb indicator
5. Magnetic compass
6. Gyro-horizon
7. Pilot direction indicator (PDI)
8. Radio compass
9. Flux gate compass
10. Manifold pressure gauge
11. Tachometers
12. Blind-landing indicator
13. Turret warning lights
14. Bomb release indicator light
15. Vacuum warning light
16. Marker beacon indicator light

17. Alarm bell switch
18. Propeller feathering circuit breakers
19. Breaker reset
20. Propeller feathering buttons
21. Keying button and recognition lights
22. Phone call switch
23. Autopilot controls
24. Bomb salvo switch
25. Formation light rheostat
26. Emergency brake levers
27. Position light switches
28. Landing lights
29. Wing flap switch
30. Landing gear light
31. Propeller speed controls
32. Turbo boost switch

33. Circuit breakers
34. Bomb-bay door warning light
35. Bomb-bay door switches and
     circuit breakers
36. Aisle stand panel light
37. Norden bombsight
38. Control column
39. Rudder pedals
40. Pilot's seat
41. Co-pilot's seat
42. Flap position indicator
43. Propeller rpm limit indicator lights
44. Landing gear indicator lights
45. Bombardier's remote gunsight

altitudes. Until the first week of fire raids proved otherwise, they were convinced antiaircraft artillery and nightfighters would scythe them down. Crews were unaware how well night cloaked them from both threats. Poor enemy radar and effective US radar jamming further diminished Japanese nighttime effectiveness.

Both precision and area night raids followed the same pattern. There were never dozens of aircraft over a city simultaneously. Even during the fire raid on Tokyo on March 9–10, there were unlikely to have been more than 12 B-29s over the city at any one time. A more typical number would have been five or six. Each aircraft took off, heading individually for the target. Bombers arrived over the target spaced at their takeoff intervals. Since B-29s typically flew between 230–290mph, a 30- to 45-second interval between takeoffs spaced bombers two to four miles apart. The distance between aircraft varied still further as pilots increased speed from the most fuel-economical 230mph to higher speeds as they approached the target area. They would not have gone to top speed, but somewhere in the range of 298–314mph would have been typical over Japan.

This meant night raids lasted one to two hours, depending on the number of aircraft attacking. Assuming nothing went wrong, it took a single wing 70 to 90 minutes to launch all of its aircraft. Multiple wings operated from different airfields. The lag between bombers taking off might have increased their time over the target from 90 minutes to two hours.

Precision nighttime raids typically targeted extremely large installations such as the Imperial Iron and Steel Works at Yawata or oil refineries and shipyards elsewhere in Japan. While the onboard radar used by B-29s in 1944 yielded poor results finding even large targets, by 1945 Superfortresses of the 315th BW were equipped with high-accuracy AN/APQ-7 Eagle radar. The downside to this system was it required a five-mile straight run to the target. This made daytime attacks using the AN/APQ-7 inadvisable. It was also risky at night if antiaircraft artillery with gun laying radar or radar-equipped nightfighters were near the bomb runs. As in other night missions, B-29s made individual runs to their target when using radar.

Fire raids began as a trickle rather than a wave. Initially, one Superfortress dropped a load of incendiaries. That first B-29, a pathfinder, carried 60+ napalm-filled 115lb M-47s which would start several dozen major fires. Some 30 to 60 seconds later, the next pathfinder dropped its bomb in an unlit part of the city near the first set of fires. Several dozen more fires then started. In another 30 to 60 seconds a third pathfinder dropped its M-47s. The process

Although pathfinder B-29s assigned to a fire raid carried 60+ 115lb M-47 incendiaries per aircraft, the majority of the Superfortresses on such a mission were laden down with nearly 1,000 six-pound M-69 incendiaries. They were clustered in E-46 containers, like the one seen here being loaded into the bomb-bay of a B-29 by armorers – the airman on the right is smoking a cigar! Each E-46 carried 47 M-69s, which scattered when the containers opened at a pre-set altitude after being dropped over the target. (NMAF)

This building was one of Tokyo's 42 main fire stations, and it was large enough to possess a firewatch tower and accommodation for up to four engines – typically 500-gallon pumpers as seen here. Although three such vehicles are visible in this photograph, most fire stations only had two. Limited in number, the engines were also small, capable of pumping only 500 gallons per minute. B-29 pathfinders leading incendiary raids had the ability to start more fires than the available engines could deal with. (Author's Collection)

duly repeated itself until the pathfinders were all through the target area.

Each fire started by an M-47 required the attention of a fire engine. An air warden with a bucket of sand could not extinguish a fire started by 115lb of napalm and white phosphorus. Within ten minutes, more than 1,000 fires demanded the attention of fire engines. Tokyo, Japan's largest city, had only 716 motorized pumper trucks, 11 fireboats, and 400 hand-drawn fire engines, leaving it overwhelmed by this initial attack on March 9–10. Other cities were far less prepared.

Soon after the last pathfinder dropped its M-47s, a B-29 carrying nearly 1,000 six-pound M-69 incendiaries released its load. Each cluster would scatter over an acre – an average of one M-69 every 43 sq ft. Some landed on pavement or dirt, but 50 percent usually hit the raid's target – typically an urban area predominantly covered by roofs, most of which could burn. At least 500 of the M-69s dropped started fires.

Although the latter was extinguishable with a bucket of sand, the available manpower could not douse all of the incendiaries before they had started blazes that could only be contained by a fire engine. Every fire engine was quickly committed, and 30 seconds later another B-29 would drop an additional 1,000 M-69s. This pattern typically went on for more than an hour.

Surprisingly, the fire raids on Japan were remarkably survivable under most circumstances. However, the March 9–10 raid turned into a horror which killed between 60,000 to 130,000 people due to a number of factors. The first was its unexpectedness. It was larger than any previous fire raid, catching people off guard. They sheltered in place, when they could have run. When they finally realized the danger they were in, it was too late to outrun the flames. The wind and relatively dry weather whipped the flames into a firestorm, a phenomenon that sucks the oxygen out of the atmosphere and creates unsurvivable blast furnace temperatures.

But a standard fire raid built slowly, drop by drop. If a healthy adult started moving towards open ground, upwind of the bombs, when the raid commenced, they could generally get to safety. A raid on Akashi, in Hyogo Prefecture, on July 7, 1945 burned out 60 percent of a city with more 80,000 inhabitants, yet only 355 people died. The city was evacuated one hour before the attack began, with one-third of the population – older adults and children – sheltering in a park north of Akashi.

Antiaircraft guns were generally effective only during the initial portion of a fire raid. After the conflagration spread communications failed, which meant antiaircraft fire could no longer be coordinated. The guns positioned closest to the target area were usually overwhelmed by flames and had to be abandoned. Furthermore, typically there were too few guns available. Tokyo had the heaviest antiaircraft defenses of any city in

XXI Bomber Command reacted to the high losses experienced during the May 24–25, 1945 fire raid on Tokyo by using a daytime strike for its final incendiary attack on the city's metropolitan area four days later. Here, bombers from the 73rd BW's 499th BG drop incendiaries – scattered by jet stream winds – on Yokohama on May 29. Escorted by P-51s and using the radar-jamming of the "Ravens," the 454 B-29s that participated in the mission were largely unmolested by fighters and antiaircraft fire. (NMAF)

Japan – 500 guns. The rest of the nation's ten largest cities had fewer, and many others had no antiaircraft artillery whatsoever. If anything was going to stop the night raids, it had to be Japan's nightfighter force.

THEORY OF NIGHTFIGHTER INTERCEPTION

In order to shoot down attacking B-29s, nightfighters had to do two things. Detect a bomber and then shoot it down, and neither was easy at night. Detection began on the ground. Both the IJAAF and the IJNAF maintained early-warning radar networks on Japan's Pacific coast and around Kyushu. The IJAAF stations had a range of 124 miles and the IJNAF stations 155 miles. This gave nightfighter crews 20–40 minutes advanced warning of an incoming raid, depending upon the target's distance from the coast. The detected position and heading of incoming enemy bombers was sent to interceptor airfields and then passed on to nightfighter crews, who were ordered to scramble.

Aircraft would be standing by ready for action because Japanese signal intelligence used the detection of pre-mission radio checks made by B-29 radiomen to give fighter crews a five-hour advance warning a raid was due. This presented interceptor airfields with the opportunity to prepare a response, with aircraft being fueled, armed, and readied for takeoff. Once aloft, the interceptors were expected to find and engage incoming bombers based on the position and heading information available at takeoff. They received no further ground guidance. During World War II, Japan never developed Ground Control Interception (GCI) systems the way Britain and Germany did, using them to guide nightfighters onto targets. GCI would have been of limited use in Japan in any case, for the IJAAF/IJNAF ground-based radar sites only reported bearing and range, not altitude.

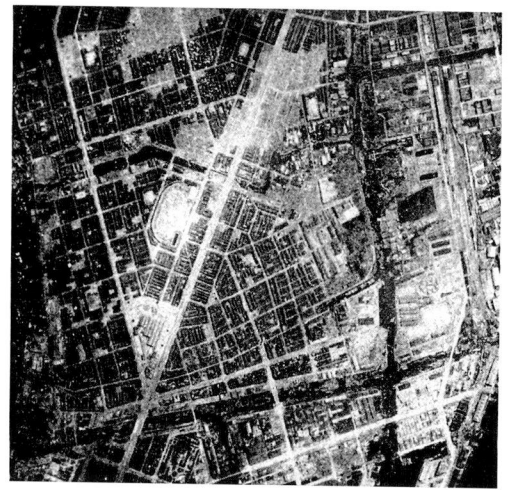
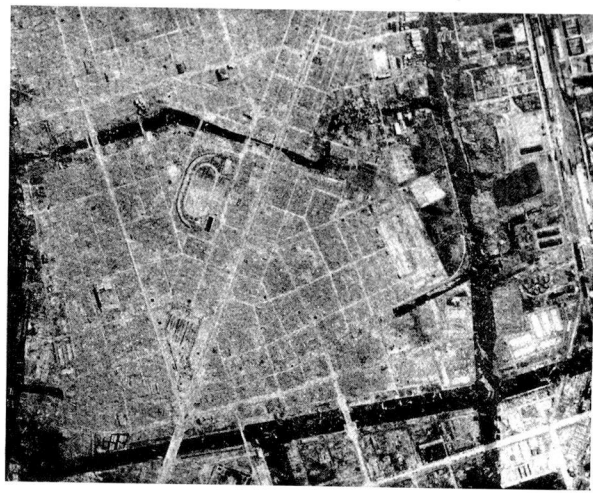

These aerial reconnaissance photographs show views of Kobe's Minato District before and after a June 1, 1945 incendiary raid. The second shot reveals the widespread devastation a fire-bombing attack could inflict on a city. Pockets of damage from a conventional bombing raid mounted on Kobe by B-29s in March can be seen in the before image. (Author's Collection)

Visually acquiring bombers was difficult enough during daylight, despite them flying in large formations that left contrails visible for miles in their wake. At night, seeking individual aircraft was quantitatively more difficult, for the naked eye saw only light and contrast in such conditions. A bright light, the moon or a star, could be seen at virtually infinite range. Similarly, aircraft showing a bright light due to exhaust glow, onboard gunfire or even cockpit lighting could be spotted miles away. Both sides went to great lengths to avoid showing such light. More common was detection due to "high contrast." A B-29 silhouetted against the moon was visible from below, while a bomber flying over a burning city would be silhouetted from above. An aircraft coned by searchlights would be similarly visible.

"High contrast" cases tended to be rare. The odds of passing a bomber flying over illuminated terrain were low, except if most of the target city was burning. Reflections of fire off the bottom of an aircraft provided only moderate contrast, while a B-29 flying through a normal dark sky would be virtually invisible until the interceptor was on top of it. Other factors reducing the crew's ability to exploit contrast detection included dirty or scratched windscreens, low oxygen levels inducing fatigue or simply poor night vision by individual pilots. Low oxygen could reduce dark perception by half, while a dirty or scratched windscreen could create confusing shadows and reflections.

Nightfighters relying on visual observation to find targets were most successful when light contrast was highest. That meant crews were most likely to find targets over a burning city or when a bomber got caught by searchlights. They were least likely to encounter the lead aircraft in a raid, with the pathfinders literally blazing a trail for follow-on bombers.

AI radar simplified finding targets, but Japanese equipment had limitations. As previously noted, radar range was just 1.86 miles in a cone roughly 9,800ft deep and 45 degrees across. A bomber flying 5,000ft above or below the radar-equipped fighter would slip past undetected, as would one broadside to or behind the nightfighter. Furthermore, only J1N1-Ss carried radar.

The key to finding targets was locating the bomber stream – the heading and altitude from which the bombers were approaching. B-29s typically passed inland

north or south of a target, turning once west of it in order to make their bomb run before heading east towards the Pacific. This gave aircraft the shortest path to safety after dropping their bombs. It also meant the heading provided to Japanese interceptors by early-warning radar was meaningless. The bombers attacked in a direction independent of their over-sea approach heading.

Nightfighters would circle the targeted city until they either detected a B-29 or the location of the bomber stream was revealed by the pattern of fires on the ground. The Japanese pilot would then fly along the bomber stream until he found a potential target to engage.

There were three favored attack methods, all dictated by the armament of the individual nightfighter. Aircraft with obliquely firing guns attacked from below and behind. These included the Ki-45 KAIc and J1N1-C/S nightfighters. A pilot flying such an aircraft started his attack by positioning the nightfighter aft and a few hundred feet below the B-29 he was targeting. Flying a parallel course below the bomber, the nightfighter crept up on the B-29 until its guns were aimed at the bomb-bay, located at the intersection of the wings and the fuselage – it was a natural aiming point. A single burst of 20mm fire here could bring down a B-29, especially if the attack was made while the aircraft was still carrying its bomb load. Even if the Superfortress had already dropped its bombs, the odds the cannon rounds would inflict fatal structural damage were high, for both the wing root and wing struts passed through the guns' target zone.

This attack had one major disadvantage. Success depended on being undetected. With a top speed of 357mph, a B-29 could outrun any Japanese nightfighter. If the latter was detected during the approach, the flight engineer would firewall the throttles and leave the attacker behind. Approaching a B-29 from the rear took several minutes, offering the bomber's crew ample time to spot their quarry.

2nd Hikotai leader Capt Jun-ichi Nakamura (left) salutes his 53rd Sentai pilots in front of their Ki-45 KAIcs at Matsudo in the spring of 1945. The unit enjoyed notable success on several nights in March, April and May during the ill-fated defense of Tokyo, with its pilots claiming a total of 32 B-29s shot down and 40 damaged. Five Toryus were in turn destroyed on the ground at Matsudo by USAAF fighters in a strafing attack on May 25. (Tony Holmes Collection)

1. Gunsight
2. Synchronizer
3. Airspeed indicator
4. Turn-and-bank indicator
5. Fore-and-aft level gauge
6. Fuel pressure gauge
7. Engine speed indicator
8. Left engine booster gauge
9. Right engine booster gauge
10. Compass
11. Altimeter
12. Oil pressure gauge
13. Gyro compass
14. Clock
15. Left engine oil temperature gauge
16. Right engine oil temperature gauge
17. Cylinder head temperature gauge
18. Exhaust temperature gauge
19. Microphone

20. Throttle controls
21. Mixture controls
22. Oil cooler shutter controls
23. Supercharger selector controls
24. Rudder pedals
25. Fuel pump
26. Cowl flaps controls
27. Status lights
28. Undercarriage position indicators
29. Ho-203 37mm cannon shell reload switch
30. Flap angle setting gauge
31. Left tank fuel selector
32. Right tank fuel selector
33. Rate gyro adjustment
34. Control column
35. Forward guns trigger
36. Oblique-firing guns trigger
37. Bomb release switch
38. Control grip

39. Pitot heat switch
40. Landing light switch
41. Landing light switch
42. Aircraft navigation lights switch
43. Aircraft navigation lights switch
44. Oil thermometer switch
45. Exhaust gas switch
46. Exhaust gas switch
47. Radio on/off switch
48. Radio talk button
49. Tailwheel locking lever
50. Boost converter
51. Generator current meter
52. Generator setting
53. Left and right electrical power switches
54. Left and right generator switches
55. Pilot's seat

Such an attack also offered several advantages. It was the easiest way to approach a B-29 undetected. Unlike the B-17 and B-24, the B-29 had no manned ball turret. The Superfortress also had no observer with a clear view of its underside, the tail gunner and two side blister gunners being tasked with watching the vulnerable underside of their aircraft. It was also a simple approach to fly, with the closing rate of the two aircraft being leisurely – 30–40mph, depending on the airspeed of the nightfighter and the B-29. At such speeds it was easy to set up an accurate shot.

The handful of J1N1-Cs fitted with obliquely firing ventral guns attacked from above and behind. As with the far more common upward-firing attack with obliquely-mounted weapons, an interception with ventral guns initially saw the Gekko positioned aft of the B-29, but in this case several hundred feet above the target. Again, the pilot crept up on the Superfortress until his guns were aimed at the intersection of the wings and the fuselage, at which point he fired.

Attacking with obliquely firing ventral guns had the same advantages and disadvantages as an interception with weapons mounted in the upper fuselage, but with one additional disadvantage. The Superfortress had an observer's blister atop the fuselage, which gave the occupant a clear view of the airspace directly above the bomber.

The third type of attack was a diving interception from above. This was limited to either Ki-45s or single-engined day fighters being used at night. In this attack, the aircraft would be flying above the bomber stream, its pilot seeking the silhouette of a B-29 illuminated by the burning city. Once a Superfortress had been spotted, the pilot would dive onto the bomber from above, opening up with his forward-firing guns as he neared the target aircraft.

This was the most difficult type of attack to make, for with a closing rate between the aircraft of 300–400mph, there was little margin for error.

If the target bomber accelerated or turned during the firing run, a miss usually resulted. Even if the attack was undetected, the chances of missing were higher than with the slower stern attacks. It did offer the advantage of surprise, however, because such attacks usually came from an unexpected direction. There was also little time for the B-29 crew to detect the nightfighter and react to the attack.

Taken from a post-war US report on Japanese air power, this crude illustration shows the USAAF assessment of how oblique attacks on B-29s were conducted. It contains several errors. The guns are shown mounted at 60 degrees from horizontal instead of 30 degrees, and the aircraft is a single-engined Ki-84 "Frank" fighter, rather than a twin-engined type such as the Ki-45 KAIc or the J1N1. Of the nocturnal encounters between nightfighters and B-29s, only one-sixth resulted in an attack on a Superfortress. Half the attacks led to no damage being inflicted on the B-29 and only 40 percent resulted in a downed aircraft. (Author's Collection)

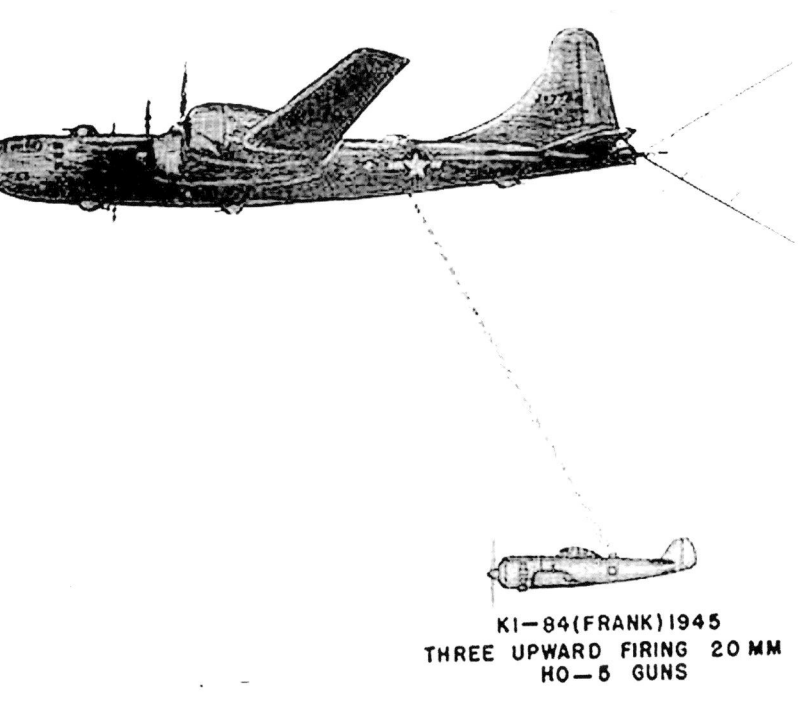

KI-84 (FRANK) 1945
THREE UPWARD FIRING 20 MM
HO-5 GUNS

This diagram shows the three distinctly different methods of attack typically used by Japanese nightfighters when engaging B-29s. They were an attack from below and behind, shooting into the bomb-bay of a B-29 with two (Ki-45 KAIc) or two/three (J1N1-S) upward-firing cannon, an attack from above and behind, shooting into the bomb-bay of a B-29 with downward-firing cannon (J1N1-S only), and a diving attack from above onto a B-29 (both Ki-45 KAIc and J1N1-S).

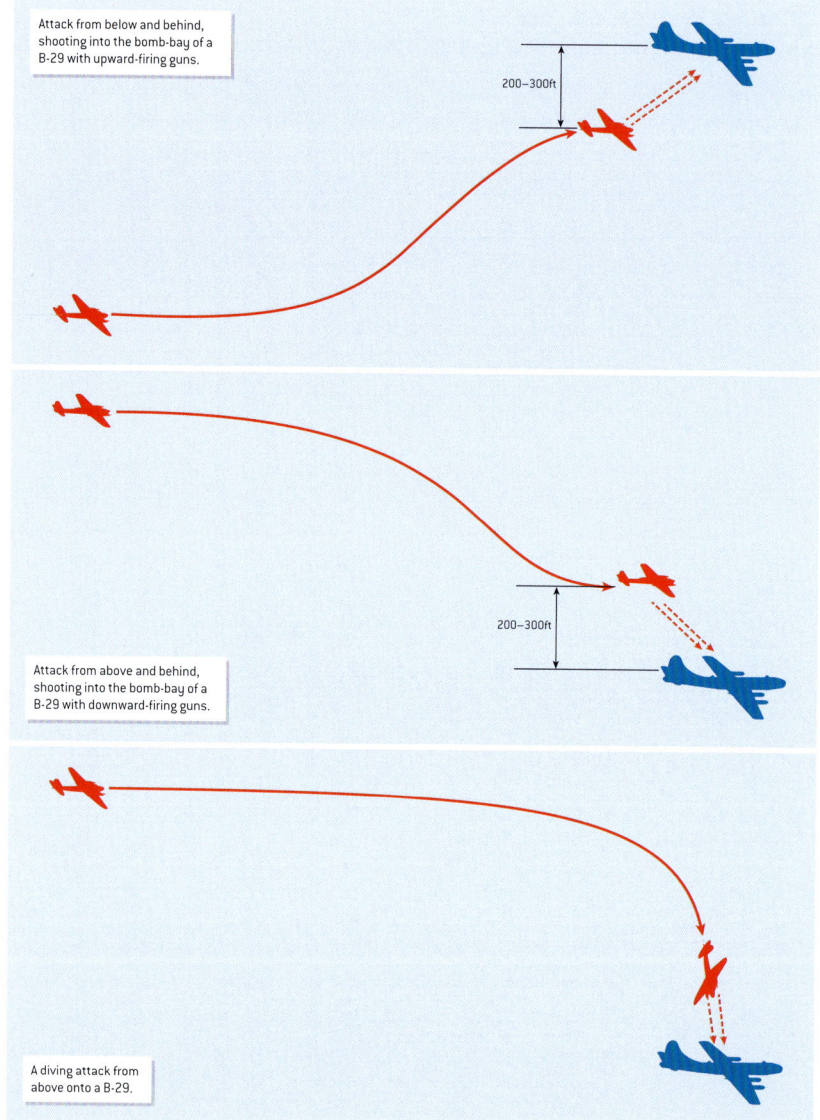

Attack from below and behind, shooting into the bomb-bay of a B-29 with upward-firing guns.

200–300ft

Attack from above and behind, shooting into the bomb-bay of a B-29 with downward-firing guns.

200–300ft

A diving attack from above onto a B-29.

NIGHTFIGHTER PILOT WASTAGE

Nightfighting was the most exacting type of aerial combat, requiring its participants to be better trained and have greater experience than pilots engaging enemy aircraft during daylight hours in typically good visibility. Bomber pilots usually stalked a city-sized target, generally flying in a straight line. Nightfighter pilots had to contend with flying in limited visibility while hunting enemy aircraft. Even a B-29 was small compared to the sky it was flying in. Nightfighters were generally multi-engined aircraft, adding another layer of complexity for pilots tasked with engaging bombers after dark.

The IJAAF and IJNAF proved reluctant to assign their top aces to multi-engined nightfighter duty, keeping them flying familiar single-engined aircraft. Both fighting forces knew the defense of the Home Islands was coming by spring 1944, and from then on the IJAAF and IJNAF slowly assembled a cadre of experienced nightfighter crews for local operations. Several of the pilots involved happened to be aces. They could have inflicted heavy losses on the B-29s once night raids started in March 1945. The problem was that few of these men, and their aircraft, were still around by then.

The B-29 campaign had begun in earnest some four months earlier, with all heavy bomber missions taking place during the day. IJAAF and IJNAF commanders committed day fighters – and their modest nightfighter force – to oppose these missions. They failed to stop the attacks, with many nightfighters and their experienced pilots being lost in this ill-fated effort. Their demise was acutely felt when Maj Gen LeMay's night bombing campaign commenced.

Having been less than impressed by Japan's air defense capabilities against daylight raids made by the B-29 force when in charge of XX Bomber Command in 1944, LeMay was contemptuous of the enemy's efforts to intercept aircraft of his XXI Bomber Command during the nocturnal campaign. He was not participating in the missions, however, even though he desperately wanted to. LeMay had been ordered not fly join his B-29 crews in raids on Japan because he had been briefed on the atomic bomb.

The crews on the flights over Japan were the ones who dealt with the risk, and their survival depended on them using the key advantages they had, namely speed and stealth. The latter was the most important, for unless a nightfighter actually spotted a Superfortress, the bomber could not be attacked. As discussed previously, visually acquiring an aircraft at night, even one as big as a B-29, was difficult.

Identifying the path of the bomber stream was the best way for the Japanese to locate bombers visually, although this was not easy for no two fire raids used the same path into a city. The Greater Tokyo Area, for example, covered approximately 5,200 square miles, allowing a multitude of possibilities. Nightfighters had to discover the bomber stream by trial and error, wasting valuable time at the onset of a raid. Even eliminating a city's burnt-out areas left a multitude of different routes into the target, all of which required coverage.

B-29s crews also learned to keep their aircraft as dark as possible. Cabin lights were switched off, instrument illumination minimized and engines set to reduce backfiring and keep exhaust glow to a minimum. If a cloud layer was near the assigned altitude range, pilots would use it to conceal their aircraft. Ground fires

Ki-45 KAIcs of 5th Sentai await their next mission at Kiyosu, southeast of Nagoya, in early 1945. This unit flew Kawasaki's twin-engined fighter for three-and-half years, during which time it saw action in the Dutch East Indies and western New Guinea, before returning to Japan to defend the Home Islands, and specifically Nagoya, in September 1944. 5th Sentai enjoyed some success against USAAF four-engined bombers, with Capt Totari Ito claiming more than 13 destroyed by war's end – some of these were B-29s. (Tony Holmes Collection)

could often be seen through a thin cloud layer, allowing enough guidance for accurate bombing – close was good enough, with bombardiers wanting to hit the dark ground between the fires.

Speed also provided safety. While B-29s were most fuel efficient at 225–235mph, once over Japanese territory the Superfortresses increased their speed so that bomb runs were made at 295–312mph. The exact speed depended on the bombload, with more ordnance slowing the aircraft. Even 295mph meant a bomber would cross the width of the Greater Tokyo Area in six to ten minutes. Since nightfighters lacked GCI support, they usually hunted over the target area only. A bomber, therefore, was typically at risk of interception for just a short time.

Speed also aided survival if the bomber was spotted by a nightfighter. The Toryu had a maximum speed of 335.5mph and the Gekko 315mph. That meant when intercepting a B-29 at 295mph, the Ki-45 enjoyed a speed advantage of 40mph and the J1N1-C/S 20mph. If the bomb run was made at 312mph, the Toryu's closing speed advantage dropped to 23mph (about the speed of a galloping horse) and the Gekko's reduced to walking pace. While bomb-run speed was not a perfect defense, it minimized opportunities for an encounter. A nightfighter pilot might find it impossible to place his aircraft in an attacking position even if the B-29's crew was oblivious to his presence.

Even when fully loaded with bombs, the Superfortress had a top speed of 348mph. If a Japanese nightfighter was detected before the aircraft attacked, the B-29 crew could firewall the throttles and outrun their opponent. It might mean the Superfortress dropped its incendiaries somewhere other than the intended target, but an optimistic crew could see that as dispersing hard-pressed firefighting efforts still further.

Maj Gen LeMay believed stealth and speed were enough to ensure B-29 safety during night missions. Originally, he wanted to send the bombers in unarmed, removing all ammunition for their guns and without the four gunners. His main reason for doing this was to increase the B-29s' bombload on the night raids. Four crewmen left on the ground freed up an extra 500lb, while the total weight of the 0.50-cal. rounds was nearly 650lb. LeMay also believed the threat posed by friendly fire – B-29s shooting each other in error – was greater than the threat posed by enemy nightfighters. Finally, defensive tracer fire signaled the presence of a Superfortress to other nightfighters. It was like lighting a flare, saying "here I am."

As noted, LeMay was not flying the missions. The crews on the flights

A B-29's primary defense against nightfighters was speed. Once its crew detected an interceptor, the aircraft could outrun it. Even fully loaded, a Superfortress had a top speed of 348mph – well above that of the Toryu or Gekko. Relying on speed was safer and simpler than shooting it out with an opponent. (NMAF)

over Japan actually dealt with the risk. For the first night raid he yielded on two points. He allowed the gunners to fly with the rest of the crew, albeit primarily as observers, and the two underside turrets to be armed. These rounds were not to be used to attack nightfighters (LeMay was still worried about friendly fire), however. The weapons were to shoot out any searchlights that caught the B-29s.

Permitting gunners to fly with their crews was initially done to maintain morale. Crews trained as a team, and leaving 40 percent of them on the ground hurt morale. Those that flew missed the presence of the men aft of the bomb-bay (only the "Raven" would have remained in the aft crew compartment if the gunners were removed). Those forced to stay on the ground felt that they were letting down the rest of the team.

Ultimately, flying with the gunners, even if the turrets were empty, proved of value. It increased survivability against nightfighters by increasing the chances a B-29 crew would spot an approaching aircraft before it could attack. Most interceptions, and the vast majority of the successful ones, were made by nightfighters approaching from astern – either above or, more typically, below the bomber. The gunners and the "Raven" (on B-29s that had ECM equipment) were the only members of the bomber's crew stationed aft of the bomb-bay. The other six were in the forward crew compartment, with no view aft. The "Raven's" station, manned during the bomb run, had no windows.

Carrying the gunners and using them as observers eliminated blind spots aft. The two side gunners watched below the B-29 on their respective sides of the aircraft. They had difficulty seeing directly below the bomber, but could manage it at a stretch. The tail gunner had an unobstructed view aft of the Superfortress. His primary focus was below and behind the bomber because that was the nightfighter's typical attack profile. The upper gunner, with an unobstructed view above the bomber, concentrated exclusively above and behind the B-29 to spot any aircraft creeping up on them from above.

The difficulties of visual acquisition faced by Japanese nightfighter pilots applied equally to the four gunners in the B-29. In fact their problems were greater because a nightfighter was one-third the size of a Superfortress. Yet the payoff from spotting a nightfighter before it attacked was significant. A B-29 that was aware it was about to be attacked could not just outrun a nightfighter, it could also maneuver. A maximum turn in either direction would spoil the aim of the intercepting pilot. This was especially true for nightfighters with obliquely firing guns. Spotting a nightfighter before it attacked virtually guaranteed that the interception would be a failure. Even a few seconds' warning could save the aircraft.

The tail gunner was the man best positioned to spot an approaching interceptor – a fighter with obliquely mounted guns had to pass through the tail gunner's field-of-view – and best positioned to attack one. After the first few night missions, B-29s were sent out with generally only the tail guns armed. The three-gun arrangement (one 20mm cannon and two 0.50-cal. machine guns) in the tail of the B-29 provided a formidable amount of firepower. Unfortunately, the bullet trajectories between the cannon and machine guns did not match, making it difficult to hit an enemy fighter with projectiles from all three weapons at the same time. (Author's Collection)

If a nightfighter was spotted approaching the Superfortress, the aircraft would immediately accelerate to outrun the interceptor, usually entering a steep turn if practical. An abrupt turn at night could cause the interceptor pilot to lose sight of the bomber. The flight engineer was responsible for the B-29's throttles, controlling the speed of the aircraft. (NMAF)

PREVIOUS PAGES

B-29 42-65281 *MISS AMERICA '62* of the 24th BS/8th BG was fleetingly targeted by an AI radar-equipped J1N1-S over Tokyo on May 24–25, 1945 during the very last nocturnal fire-bombing mission to target Tokyo. The nightfighter had been spotted by an alert gunner just prior to the patient Gekko pilot opening fire. The bomber, which had presented itself as a tempting target when flying straight and level, abruptly turned and sped up. Knowing his J1N1-S could not keep up with an alerted bomber, the IJNAF pilot hurriedly took his shot. The 20mm rounds fired from the obliquely mounted Type 99 cannon arced skyward, missing the fuselage. A few shells struck the port wing outboard of the No. 1 engine, but these were not enough to inflict fatal damage to the Superfortress. *MISS AMERICA '62* made it home to Tinian, and eventually completed more than 50 missions by war's end. Serving as a weather reconnaissance aircraft, target tug and, finally, a range target, the veteran bomber somehow avoided destruction and has been an exhibit in the Travis Air Force Base Museum in California since the late 1980s.

After the first round of firebombing raids, LeMay stopped arming the lower turrets but provided ammunition for the tail turret instead. This allowed the tail gunner to attack nightfighters approaching from behind. Whether an aircraft was closing from below and behind or above and behind, the tail gunner could usually engage it.

ECM was rarely useful against nightfighters. The radar jammers were tuned to the frequency used by Japanese ground-based radar, not AI radar. B-29s carried no radar detectors. Even if they had, few Japanese nightfighters had AI radar. If B-29s had had radar detectors they could have been counterproductive, lulling crews into a false sense of security. The "Raven" would have been listening for a non-existent radar bounce. Meanwhile, a fighter without radar could approach unseen to make an attack.

EVASIVE FLYING

One tactic B-29 pilots used to protect against nightfighter attack was to fly an evasive course over the target area. Like a convoy zig-zagging to avoid submarines, making "S-turns" over a Japanese city being bombed threw off a stalking nightfighter. At worst it affected their aim, and at best a turn would cause the nightfighter to lose the bomber entirely.

Aircraft with obliquely firing guns were effective only against B-29s flying straight and level. Random turns were an effective defense against these types of attack.

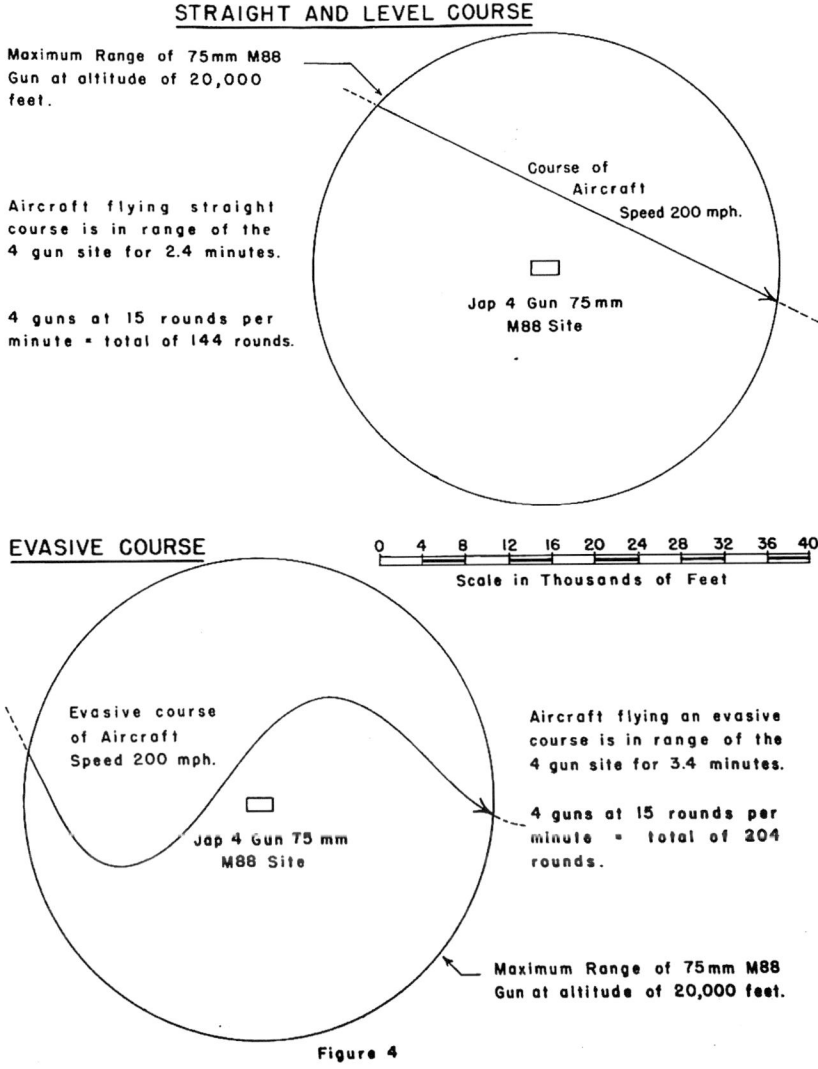

STRAIGHT AND LEVEL COURSE

Maximum Range of 75mm M88 Gun at altitude of 20,000 feet.

Course of Aircraft Speed 200 mph.

Aircraft flying straight course is in range of the 4 gun site for 2.4 minutes.

Jap 4 Gun 75mm M88 Site

4 guns at 15 rounds per minute = total of 144 rounds.

EVASIVE COURSE

0 4 8 12 16 20 24 28 32 36 40
Scale in Thousands of Feet

Evasive course of Aircraft Speed 200 mph.

Aircraft flying an evasive course is in range of the 4 gun site for 3.4 minutes.

Jap 4 Gun 75 mm M88 Site

4 guns at 15 rounds per minute = total of 204 rounds.

Maximum Range of 75mm M88 Gun at altitude of 20,000 feet.

Figure 4
Increase in Number of Rounds Fired when Evasive Course is followed

This illustration from a Twentieth Air Force manual reflects the official position on evasive maneuvering over the target. (Author's Collection)

Unexpected turns could easily cause a nightfighter pilot to lose sight of a target bomber. At night, this frequently resulted in the pursuing pilot losing the target permanently. Yet while "S-turns" were effective, such maneuvers were officially discouraged by XXI Bomber Command. Its view (as illustrated in the diagram reproduced in this chapter from an XXI Bomber Command combat crew manual) was that evasive maneuvers made the bomber more vulnerable to antiaircraft fire because it kept the B-29 within range of ground fire for 50 percent longer. Minimizing the time spent over a target was a rational choice in an environment thick with antiaircraft guns.

Opposition from antiaircraft guns was greatest at the start of a fire raid, before the conflagration spread, and it declined as the raid continued. Spreading fires burned out antiaircraft batteries and ground radars. Conversely, the risk of being attacked by a nightfighter was lowest at the raid's onset, before the bomber stream was identified and when skies over the target were darkest. It grew as the mission continued. The bomber stream's location could then be identified as growing fires better illuminated the bombers. B-29 crews knew that. Pathfinders might fly straight in and out, but at some point during the raid follow-on pilots would decide that the risk of increased antiaircraft fire was outweighed by the growing threat posed by nightfighters, resulting in them disregarding command guidance about maneuvering.

BOMBERS AND NIGHTFIGHTERS IN ACTION

Ki-45 KAIcs of 53rd Sentai stand ready to protect the Home Islands from Matsudo in 1944–45. The muzzles of the obliquely mounted twin 20mm Ho-5 cannon can be clearly seen protruding from the upper fuselage of the aircraft in the foreground. The unit's Toryus exhibit a number of different camouflage schemes and individual markings. The white bands around the hinomaru indicate that 53rd Sentai was a home defense unit. (Author's Collection)

Japan began preparing to defend its homeland in early 1944, transferring fighter Kokutai from various theaters back to the Home Islands and reorganizing their deployment. By June of that year, the IJAAF had divided Japan into five sectors. Four regions (Hokkaido and northern Honshu, the Kanto region around Tokyo, Osaka and Kure, and Shimonoseki) were assigned Shidan (flying divisions), while Nagoya was guarded by a smaller Hikodan (flying brigade).

By June, all three southern Shidan had at least one nightfighter Sentai (regiment) assigned, theoretically equipped with 24 Ki-45 KAIcs. 53rd Hiko Sentai protected Tokyo, while two Sentai, comprising 4th Hiko Sentai, guarded Shimonoseki. A further Sentai covered Osaka. Nagoya did not have IJAAF nightfighters, while Hokkaido was given an understrength Chutai (squadron). Usually less than half the Kai-45s assigned to a unit were airworthy. The IJNAF also organized 302nd Kokutai at Yokosuka, 38 miles due south of Tokyo, on March 1, 1944, which had 24 J1N1-Cs on strength (only nine were airworthy). This unit, which moved to Atsugi just weeks after its formation, was also equipped with Mitsubishi J2M Raiden single-seat fighters.

The first encounter between B-29s and Japanese nightfighters occurred in the early morning hours of June 16, 1944 when the 58th BW sent 75 B-29s from Chinese airfields on a night raid against the Imperial Iron and Steel Works at Yawata, which produced one-quarter of Japan's rolled steel. The works was well-protected, guarded not only by 4th Hiko

Sentai but also by Kawasaki Ki-61 Hien-equipped 59th Hiko Sentai. Yawata was also ringed by searchlight units.

Japanese radar detected the incoming B-29s at 2331 hrs on June 15, and an air raid alarm sounded at 0024 hrs. Twenty-four Ki-45s were scrambled, taking off from 0027 hrs to patrol the skies over Yawata. The subsequent results of the mission reflected poorly on both sides. B-29s began reaching Yawata at 0038 hrs, and over the next two hours 47 Superfortresses dropped bombs on the Imperial Iron and Steel Works – 15 visually and 32 using radar. Seven other bombers hit alternate targets, while the rest either aborted or crashed en route. Antiaircraft fire was heavy, but inaccurate. The searchlights were ineffective. Only a few Ki-45s found the B-29s, and one Toryu claimed a bomber shot down. All other contacts were fruitless, the Ki-45 crews being unable to make attacks on the fast-flying Superfortresses. Nevertheless, Toryu pilots claimed eight B-29s downed and four damaged.

The 58th BW lost seven bombers, but only one to a Ki-45. Two crashed on takeoff or while flying to the target, and two were brought down by antiaircraft fire or mechanical failure. Another bomber suffered engine failure and landed on an airfield in mainland China that was within range of IJAAF aircraft. They soon destroyed it on the ground. A seventh crashed flying a bomb damage assessment photo-reconnaissance flight the following day. On this occasion, Superfortress bombing proved as ineffective as the Japanese nightfighter force. Of the 107 tons of ordnance dropped, just one 500lb bomb hit the Imperial Iron and Steel Works complex.

The Yawata raid and US landings at Saipan in June–July 1944 (which eventually gave the USAAF a base within B-29 range of Japan) led to the IJNAF increasing its Home Islands air defense capabilities. To protect bases at Sasebo and Kure, it added J1N1-equipped nightfighter elements to 332nd Kokutai and 352nd Kokutai, respectively, in August 1944.

XX Bomber Command launched five more night raids against Japan from China in 1944. The first two, on Sasebo on July 7 and Omura, in Nagasaki, on August 10, saw naval bases targeted by 14 and 24 B-29s, respectively. An aircraft factory in Omura was then attacked on four separate occasions – once in October, twice in November and once in December. No bombers were lost to antiaircraft fire or nightfighters (which failed to intercept either raid) during the attacks on July 7 and August 10. One bomber ditched while returning home, however.

The October 25 raid on Omura was a large affair, with 58 B-29s being sent. They seriously damaged the factory, and all the bombers returned safely. Two aircraft were lost per raid on the November 5 and 11 missions, all apparently due to damage inflicted by antiaircraft fire. In each raid one aircraft was shot down and one diverted to Vladivostok, in the USSR, where it was interned. A third follow-up mission to Omura, on December 19, with 17 B-29s seems to have suffered the loss of one aircraft to a nightfighter.

These raids, and a final China-based mission to Nagasaki on the night of January 6, 1945 with 48 B-29, were again inconclusive in respect to results for either side. The bombers failed to hit their targets and virtually all of the Ki-45s sent to intercept the B-29s failed to find the enemy. By then, Japanese attention was beginning to shift away from Kyushu and southwestern Honshu after airfields in the Marianas had started to receive Superfortresses in October 1944.

Lt(jg) Sachio Endo (left foreground) was one of Japan's first home defense nightfighter aces. Flying with both 302nd and 352nd Kokutai, he was credited with shooting down eight B-29s and damaging eight more mostly during the fall of 1944 – this total also includes victories achieved during daylight. Endo and his observer, CPO Ozaki, were killed on January 14, 1945 when their Gekko burst into flames and crashed after being hit by defensive fire from B-29s over Enshu Nada. (Author's Collection)

From November 24, 1944, Pacific-based B-29s of XXI Bomber Command began attacking Japanese cities. Tokyo was the initial target, and the main focus for the next several months, although Osaka, Kobe, and Nagoya were also struck. These were the most heavily defended targets in Japan, with two nightfighter units in Tokyo (one IJAAF and one IJNAF), one IJAAF unit in Osaka and one IJNAF unit in Hiroshima (at Kure). Two nightfighter units at Omura and Fukouoka guarded Kyushu. Tokyo, with 24 Ki-45s and 24 J1N1s headquartered at Tachikawa and Atsugi, respectively, boasted the largest concentration of nightfighters in Japan.

Not all of these aircraft were airworthy, however, and combat attrition also affected unit strength from December 1944. The Japanese had tried to conserve their modest nightfighter force during the first month of the Marianas-based bombing campaign – all raids flown by XXI Bomber Command initially took place during the daytime. But when single-engined fighters failed to inflict significant losses on the unescorted bombers, both the IJAAF and the IJNAF began committing nightfighters to the fray.

Such a tactic had worked on August 20, 1944, when XX Bomber Command mounted a daylight raid on Yawata. The USAAF lost 12 of the 88 B-29s sortied, with two of the Superfortresses falling to 302nd Kokutai pilot Lt(jg) Sachio Endo in a J1N1 from 352nd Kokutai – he also claimed a third bomber as a probable and two more damaged. Endo would ultimately be credited with eight B-29s shot down and eight damaged, all during daylight interceptions, prior to his Gekko being hit while attacking more Superfortresses over Enshu Nada on January 14, 1945. Both he and his observer, CPO Ozaki, were killed.

The Yawata results of August 20 proved a one-off. The Ki-45 and J1N1 were larger and slower than their single-engined fighter counterparts, making oblique attacks from behind suicidal during daylight, when the Toryu and Gekko could be easily seen by B-29 gunners as they slowly crept up on a formation. Furthermore, the heavy fighters only had one or two forward-firing guns, which gave them less firepower than dedicated day interceptors. Nightfighter pilots, desperate to down a B-29, resorted to head-on attacks and even ramming. Fighter attrition was tremendous, with no commensurate increase in B-29 losses.

Both the IJAAF and the IJNAF focused on short-term goals, perhaps deciding that there would be no increase in the number of night raids flown from the Marianas – very few were undertaken through to the end of February 1945. Then on March 9–10, 1945, recently arrived Maj Gen LeMay switched XXI Bomber Command almost exclusively to night bombing. Only 14 of the 325 B-29s sent to Tokyo that night were lost. Antiaircraft fire was

confirmed as having downed one bomber and damaged a second so badly that it was scrapped. Five others ditched due to fuel or mechanical problems. Seven were lost to unknown causes, with most of them probably falling to antiaircraft fire or possibly to the firestorm winds raised by the raid – several returning aircraft reported being flipped by updrafts. The late and anemic nightfighter reaction made it unlikely that any B-29s were lost to Ki-45s or J1N1s.

The results of the next five night raids were no better for the IJAAF or IJNAF. They all took place over a nine-day span, with at least 300 bombers attacking on each occasion. Total US losses were seven aircraft – four were to unknown causes, two of which were perhaps due to nightfighter attacks. Ki-45 crews flying from Osaka and Kobe reported just 93 nightfighter attacks over the latter city during these significant raids, reflecting that the IJAAF had not yet adjusted to the new tactics being employed by XXI Bomber Command.

April and May saw the battle between B-29s and nightfighters climax over the Tokyo region. Two raids on the capital in April cost XXI Bomber Command 20 Superfortresses, with as many as nine falling to nightfighters – three on April 13 and six just two nights later. However, nearly 350 B-29s were sent on each raid, so these losses were negligible. On May 25–26, 464 B-29s fire-bombed Tokyo and 26 aircraft were lost – the highest number downed during the campaign.

Both the IJAAF and IJNAF had thrown everything they had, including day fighters, against the Superfortresses. Conditions were optimal for visual acquisition, with a three-quarter moon illuminating the sky. Of the 26 Superfortresses lost, 16 were claimed by nightfighters. The most successful pilot was SFPO Juzo Kuramoto, with observer Ens Shiro Kurotori, of Yokosuka Kokutai. Actual losses to nightfighters may have been only slightly less than the 16 credited, with little claim inflation. Some 100

In a daylight confrontation between a B-29 and a Japanese nightfighter, a Ki-45 Toryu makes a head-on pass at a bomber from the 29th BG. The high closing rate and single forward-firing gun carried by the Toryu made a hit unlikely. This was a typical result when crews of these aircraft met in combat. Frustrated with their efforts to shoot bombers down, some IJAAF crews resorted to ramming. (NMAF)

Ground support personnel from Yokosuka Kokutai pose with a pilot (possibly ace Ens Shigetoshi Kudo) in front of a radar-equipped J1N1-S in the early spring of 1945. This aircraft was marked with eight victory symbols on the fuselage just forward of the tail section – Kudo was credited with eight aircraft shot down in 1942–43 while serving with 251st Kokutai in the South Pacific. (Author's Collection)

Newly promoted WO Juzo Kuramoto of Yokosuka Kokutai reads the commendation he received from the Commander-in-Chief of Yokosuka Naval Station following his extraordinary efforts in the defense of Tokyo on the night of May 25–26, 1945, when he and his observer, Ens Shiro Kurotori, claimed five B-29s destroyed in a single mission. (Tony Holmes Collection)

B-29s returned with battle damage, one third from nightfighter attacks. Kuramoto's J1N1-S was specially modified, being radar-equipped and fitted with three obliquely-firing 20mm cannon. It is highly plausible that Kuramoto and Kurotori did indeed spot and shoot down five B-29s in a two-hour period, only breaking off their pursuit of the bombers when they ran low on fuel.

Having initially served as a Mitsubishi G4M Rikko medium bomber pilot, Kuramoto had returned to Japan in December 1943 to convert to nightfighters. Joining Yokosuka Kokutai two months later, he was heavily involved in experimentation with radar-equipped J1N1-Cs. Such flying gave Kuramoto a clear advantage over his contemporaries during the spring of 1945, and with Ens Shiro Kurotori in the Gekko's rear cockpit, he claimed his first B-29 victory (and a second bomber damaged) over the Kanto area on the night of April 15. Following his outstanding haul on May 25–26, Kuramoto was presented with a commendation and a ceremonial sword from the Commander-in-Chief of Yokosuka Naval Station. He was also promoted two ranks to warrant officer – a rare honor for a servicemen who was still alive. Kuramoto subsequently failed to add to his tally of six victories before war's end.

Nightfighters were effective only when cities (Tokyo, Osaka and Kobe) near their airfields were attacked, and most of these key targets had been burned out by May 27. LeMay then switched to daytime incendiary raids, with B-29s escorted by P-51 Mustangs, for the unburnt parts of those cities. Night raids continued elsewhere. Japanese commanders, chastened by the failure of their maximum effort on May 25–26, decided to conserve their remaining nightfighters. Some still sortied, but most were kept on the ground, both to preserve fuel and to be available when the inevitable invasion started. B-29s were occasionally still lost to nightfighters through to war's end, but only one or two at a time.

STATISTICS AND
ANALYSIS

The Twentieth Air Force's XX and XXI Bomber Commands flew 144 night combat missions over Japan with B-29s during 1944–45 – eight from Chinese bases and 136 from the Marianas. There were 14,845 sorties (individual aircraft flying to the target), with an average of 103 B-29s sent on each mission. Total losses from all causes during those missions were 138 bombers, an average of just under one B-29 per mission. That gave an individual B-29 crewman a 0.9 percent chance of going down on a night mission, or a 72 percent chance of surviving a 35-mission tour.

His chances of being shot down by a Japanese nightfighter were even smaller. Ki-45s and J1N1s probably shot down only 33 B-29s between them during night raids – just under a quarter of all Superfortress losses. Even assuming that *all* bombers lost for unknown reasons during nocturnal missions were nightfighter casualties raises the total to just 53 aircraft. That assumes Japanese antiaircraft fire was totally ineffective and nightfighters were present over cities far from the airfields at which they were based.

The 33 victories assigned to nightfighters is an estimate. It adds known nightfighter victories to a fraction of unknown cause losses. The fraction was determined based on reported nightfighter sightings and attacks reported post-mission by B-29 crews, and the ratio damage to returning aircraft caused by antiaircraft fire and nightfighters, respectively. Three-quarters of the B-29s returning battle-damaged had been hit by antiaircraft fire during night missions. Only a quarter had been damaged by nightfighters. It seems likely that aircraft lost through enemy action split the cause roughly by the same proportions – three bombers downed by antiaircraft fire for every one shot down by nightfighters.

Even Japanese sources concede the relative ineffectiveness of the nightfighters. The battle for the Home Islands saw only ten nightfighter pilots become aces, and their combined total of claimed victories was 67. That tally was almost certainly exaggerated (fighter pilot claims typically are, regardless of side, sometimes spectacularly so). Claimed kills often exceeded the total number of bombers lost for that mission. Those tallies may also include B-29s downed by nightfighters during daylight missions.

While nightfighters were a risk to be faced, they were not the greatest cause of B-29 losses. Operational failure – mechanical issues, fuel exhaustion and landing and takeoff accidents – generated significantly more losses than did Japanese nightfighters, which were a manageable risk for the Twentieth Air Force. This particular Superfortress was lost on Iwo Jima's South Field on April 25, 1945 when it was struck by P-51D 44-63993 of the 45th FS/15th FG after the fighter suffered engine failure during its landing approach. [NMAF]

Regardless, it paints a picture of nightfighter failure, with results vindicating Maj Gen LeMay's contempt for Japan's nightfighter capability. There were several main reasons for this failure. The most important was operational. Japan's lack of GCI proved fatal. Britain, Germany, and the United States successfully used GCI. A nightfighter cannot shoot a bomber down if it cannot find it. GCI vectored nightfighters to a target. It worked best with AI radar-equipped nightfighters, but even pilots relying on visual acquisition benefitted for it brought them to a patch of sky occupied by the enemy. A pilot then knew *something* was close.

There were several reasons for Japan's failure to use GCI. Both the IJAAF and the IJNAF lacked the radar network to support it, and the radars they did have were inadequate. Their early warning systems pointed outward. Ground-based radars in Japan's interior were used primarily for gun laying – directing the fire of antiaircraft artillery. More importantly, GCI required a central control center to receive radar data and correlate it. Japan never developed such a center. IJAAF–IJNAF rivalry prevented cooperative efforts, but individual services neglected building their own control centers in any case.

Lacking GCI, nightfighter pilots were very much on their own once aloft. Those without radar depended on chance to locate a target. Radar-equipped aircraft were more likely to find bombers, since they could reliably detect anything within their search cone of 1.86 miles. For both, the chance was so low that contact was only likely during massive raids when hundreds of bombers passed over the target area, and only over the target area. It was virtually impossible to find a bomber before it entered the target area or after it had departed.

An issue that affected both operational and technical capabilities when it came to detecting B-29s was the poor quality of Japanese radar equipment. As other Allied and Axis air arms showed over and over again, reliable radar was critical for successful nightfighter operations, yet Japanese systems had several limitations. All ground-based early-warning and gun laying radars operated in the same narrow frequency band, even though IJAAF and IJNAF equipment had been developed independently. This made them easy to jam. Furthermore, Japanese early warning radar did not provide altitude information. An altitude difference greater than 5,000ft between bomber and interceptor rendered the former effectively invisible to the latter. During the first round of nighttime fire raids, bombers used an unexpectedly low altitude. The nightfighters aloft circled at the wrong height above them, leaving the first bombers to attack their target free from aerial interception.

The IJNAF's AI radar was inadequate in three ways. It was short-ranged, mechanically unreliable and available in limited quantities. As previously noted, the IJAAF failed to field such equipment. Even the earliest US AI radar had a range twice that of the systems used by IJNAF nightfighters in 1945. The American SCR-720 radar, employed by USAAF nightfighters, had a range more than five times that of the IJNAF's FD-2. Furthermore, the SCR-720 entered service in 1943.

Prone to breakdowns, the FD-2 was still an experimental system at the start of 1945, and all of the units installed on J1N1-Ss were hand-built

pre-production items, as were the components used in them. Component quality was also questionable and assembly errors common, while operators were inexperienced and poorly trained. Despite these limitations, when the FD-2 did work, it provided a decided advantage to a J1N1-S pilot. There were never enough FD-2s available, however. No more than 100 sets were produced between November 1944 and war's end, which meant that only a handful of Gekkos received them. None were installed in Ki-45s because the Toryu was an IJAAF aircraft. The IJNAF was unwilling to share sets, or its technical knowledge, with IJAAF radar developers.

Another reason for failure were the aircraft Japan used as nightfighters. Their design dated to the mid-1930s. They were too slow to effectively intercept B-29s and could not carry a battery of weapons large enough to guarantee a kill when they did intercept a Superfortress. Both the Toryu and the Gekko were slower than the B-29. The top speed of the latter was barely above the bomb-run speed of the Superfortress. If it detected a B-29 on radar at a distance of less than two miles, the pursuit to attack range could consume 30 minutes. Even a Toryu, with its higher speed, required three to five minutes to line up an attack. That gave the B-29's gunners time to spot an approaching interceptor, at which point the game was up. The bomber would go to top speed and outrun the fighter. The only successful nightfighter attacks were the result of undetected ambushes.

Even when the interceptor made a textbook approach, it could only fire two 20mm cannon at the target. A perfectly aimed burst would bring down a B-29, but that rarely happened. Thirty-four Superfortresses returned from missions after being damaged by nightfighters, which implies that a B-29 had a good chance of surviving even a successful nightfighter attack.

By contrast, US nightfighters typically were armed with either four 20mm cannon, six 0.50-cal. machine guns or two 20mm cannon and four 0.50-cal. machine guns. SFPO Juzo Kuramoto's successful downing of five B-29s in one night was achieved in a J1N1-S experimentally armed with three obliquely firing 20mm cannon.

A final factor in the nightfighter's lack of success was an insufficient number of available aircraft. Soviet leader Joseph Stalin once said, "Quantity has a quality all its own." The Japanese nightfighter campaign against the B-29 illustrates what he meant. There were not enough nightfighters to defeat the B-29s of the Twentieth Air Force. In June 1944, when XX Bomber Command struck Yawata, the IJAAF had 200 fighters

The fires started in Tokyo during the predawn hours of March 10, 1945 continued burning well after the sun had risen on that day. Photo-reconnaissance F-13A Superfortresses captured the scope of the destruction wrought by the incendiary bombs in this photograph. Smoke rose from the burned-out sections of Tokyo (clearly visible here in the center and bottom right) late into the following day. (LOC)

A6M5s and J1N1-Ss of 302nd Kokutai share the flightline at Atsugi in 1945. A solitary D4Y2-S Suisei nightfighter can also be seen taxiing past at the extreme right. Although the unit was supposed to have as many as 24 Gekkos on strength, as well as 48 single-seat fighters, it rarely had more than 15 J1N1s available at any one time. These shared the nightfighter mission with two Gingas and six Suiseis, although the latter types proved to be of questionable value in the fight against B-29s. (Tony Holmes Collection)

Three J1N1-Ss, each equipped with FD-2 AI radar (and associated antennas), are surrounded by G4M3 "Betty" bombers and D4Y2/3 "Judy" dive-bombers – as well as two ultra-rare J5N1 Tenrai twin-engined fighters – at Yokosuka Naval Air Base in September 1945. As per the Allies' surrender directives issued to the Japanese military, all aircraft have had their propellers and spinners removed so as to prevent any one-off kamikaze attacks by maverick aircrew. A solitary C6N1 "Myrt" reconnaissance aircraft can also be seen, as well as a K5Y "Willow" biplane trainer that has had the Hinomaru cut out from its upper wing fabric by souvenir hunters. (NHHC)

assigned to the defense of the Home Islands. The IJNAF had just 18. When XXI Bomber Command commenced its campaign against Japan in November 1944, these numbers had increased to 375 and 125, respectively. Roughly one-third of the IJAAF fighters, around 124 aircraft – were Ki-45s. The IJNAF had 72 J1N1-C/Ss shared between three Kokutai.

While the total number of fighters increased by one-third between January and August 1945, the nightfighter numbers actually declined after Toryu and Gekko production ceased in December 1944. Both types were supposed to have been replaced by newer aircraft, but the latter never went into production. Losses had to be made up from aircraft held in reserve.

Moreover, the aircraft were geographically distributed. There were never more than 60 nightfighters defending Tokyo, and only 30 to 40 each at Osaka and Hiroshima. Those numbers reflected the *total* number of aircraft present, not the numbers that were flyable. On November 11, 1944, 302nd Kokutai had 24 J1N1s, of which only nine were airworthy. Typically, one-third to one-half of all nightfighters were unserviceable, especially after January 1945 when battle damage increased the number of aircraft undergoing repair.

There were probably no more than 30 nightfighters aloft during the air battle fought over Tokyo on May 25–26, 1945. Roughly one B-29 went down for every two nightfighters available. Had the Japanese been able to put up 90 Ki-45s and J1N1s that night, bomber losses would have doubled – close to the ten percent loss ratio viewed as unsustainable by the USAAF. This suggests that despite the handicaps plaguing Japanese nightfighters, had Ki-45 KAIcs and J1N1-Ss been available in strength, the IJAAF and IJNAF could have stopped the nighttime fire raids.

AFTERMATH

The Empire of Japan surrendered unconditionally on August 15, 1945. It took Emperor Hirohito's personal intervention to force the military to accept surrender. Some, like Capt Yasuna Kozono, were determined to fight on regardless. An attempted coup by die-hards first had to be quashed, but the Emperor's will prevailed.

Although two atomic bombs and a Soviet declaration of war remain the most common explanation for the Japanese defeat, XXI Bomber Command played a major role in forcing the enemy to surrender. Its raids had left the country's industrial base in ruins, and the mines the B-29s dropped starved the Japanese population of food and its industries of raw resources. The failure of the IJAAF and IJNAF (and specifically its nightfighters) to stop the Twentieth Air Force undertaking night incendiary raids and mining missions allowed XXI Bomber Command to prevail.

Gen Douglas MacArthur, who had only just been made Supreme Commander for the Allied Powers, flew in to Atsugi on August 30, 1945, preparatory to formally accepting Japan's surrender on board the battleship USS *Missouri* (BB-63) in Tokyo Bay on September 2. This airfield was home to J1N1-equipped 302nd Kokutai, one of the IJNAF's premier fighter groups that had been tasked with defending Tokyo. MacArthur's arrival marked the start of the base's transition initially into a major USAAF airfield and then a naval air station for US Navy units forward-deployed to Japan. Eventually, it became Naval Air Facility Atsugi, a joint US–Japanese naval air base.

This was the fate that befell most of the Twentieth Air Force's combat-veteran B-29s. Stripped of their engines, these aircraft have been unceremoniously dumped in a scrapyard on Tinian. (NMAF)

J1N1-S construction number 7334 (which was subsequently handed over to the Smithsonian National Air and Space Museum) is prepared for flight testing and evaluation by the USAAF's Flight Test Section in June 1946. Having been shipped to the USA on board the escort carrier *Barnes* in November–December 1945, the aircraft was returned to airworthiness by the Maintenance Division at Middletown Air Depot in Harrisburg, Pennsylvania. (Tony Holmes Collection)

The Japanese military was dismantled after the official Instrument of Surrender was signed. Its equipment was scrapped, including all military aircraft. The only survivors were those taken by nations it occupied in World War II for use in their air forces (which included a few Ki-45s incorporated into China's Nationalist Air Force). The USAAF and US Navy also rounded up 145 aircraft for technical evaluation and shipped them to the United States.

The victorious Twentieth Air Force and its B-29s experienced a similar, if less drastic, draw down. The Superfortress remained in the inventory of both the USAAF and its successor, the US Air Force, until 1960. Most of the Superfortresses used post-war were ones which had never left the US prior to war's end. Many of the aircraft that actually flew combat missions were scrapped on the Marianas.

Today, of 3,970 B-29s built, just 22 remain – two in flyable condition. All bar two are in the United States. There is one on static display in Britain's Imperial War Museum at Duxford, in Cambridgeshire, and another in South Korea's KAI Aerospace Museum in Sacheon. The other 20 are scattered around the United States on display, in storage or undergoing restoration.

Only two examples of Japanese nightfighters exist, one Ki-45 KAIc and one J1N1-C. Both are in the Smithsonian National Air and Space Museum in Virginia. They were among the Japanese aircraft shipped to the United States onboard the escort carrier USS *Barnes* (CVE-20). The J1N1-C has been fully restored and is on display at the National Air and Space Museum's Steven F. Udvar-Hazy Center in Chantilly, Virginia. The fuselage of the Ki-45 is also displayed within the Steven F. Udvar-Hazy Center. Its wings, however, remain in storage at the Paul E. Garber Preservation, Restoration, and Storage Facility in Suitland, Maryland.

The world's only surviving examples of the Ki-45 and J1N1 have been on display in the Smithsonian National Air and Space Museum's Steven F. Udvar-Hazy Center for 20 years. Although the Gekko was fully restored more than four decades ago, only the fuselage of its Ki-45 (shown here) is presently on display. The rest of the aircraft remains in storage. (Wikipedia)

FURTHER READING

Anderton, David A., Aggressors, *Volume 3 – Interceptor vs Heavy Bomber* (Howell Press, Inc., 1991)

Claringbould, Michael John, *Pacific Profiles Volume 1 – Japanese Army Fighters, New Guinea & the Solomons 1942–1944* (Avonmore Books, 2020)

Claringbould, Michael John, *Pacific Profiles Volume 13 – IJN Bombers, Transports, Flying Boats & Miscellaneous Types, South Pacific 1942–1944* (Avonmore Books, 2024)

Craven, Wesley Frank and Cate, James Lea (editors), *The Army Air Forces In World War II, Volume Five – The Pacific: Matterhorn to Nagasaki, June 1944 to August 1945* (Office of Air Force History, 1983)*

Craven, Wesley Frank and Cate, James Lea (editors), *The Army Air Forces In World War II, Volume Six – Men and Planes* (Office of Air Force History, 1983)*

Francillon, René J., *Japanese Aircraft of the Pacific War* (Putnam, 1970)

Hansell, Haywood S., *The Strategic Air War Against Germany And Japan – A Memoir* (Office of Air Force History, United States Air Force, 1986)*

Hata, Ikuhiko, Izawa, Yasuho and Shores, Christopher, *Japanese Army Air Force Fighter Units and their Aces 1931–1945* (Grub Street, 2002)

Hata, Ikuhiko, Izawa, Yasuho and Shores, Christopher, *Japanese Naval Air Force Fighter Units and their Aces 1932–1945* (Grub Street, 2011)

LeMay, Curtis E., *Combat Crew Manual, XX Bomber Command* (APO 493, December 1944)*

LeMay, Curtis E. and Yenne, Bill, *Superfortress – The Story of the B-29 and American Air Power* (Berkley Books, 1989)

Mann, Robert A., *The B-29 Superfortress – A Comprehensive Registry of the Planes and Their Missions* (McFarland & Company, Inc., 2004)

Mikesh, Robert C. and Tagaya, Osamu, *Moonlight Interceptor – Japan's "Irving" Night Fighter* (Smithsonian Institution Press, 1985)

Morgan, Robert K. and Powers, Ron, *The Man Who Flew the Memphis Belle – Memoir of a WWII Bomber Pilot* (New American Library, 2002)

Operational Archives, US Naval History Division, *Reports of the U.S. Naval Technical Mission to Japan, 1945–1946* (US Naval History Division, 1974)*

Price, Alfred, *Instruments of Darkness – The History of Electronic Warfare, 1939–1945* (Frontline Books, 2017)

United States Strategic Bombing Survey, Effects of Incendiary Bomb Attacks on Japan – A Report on Eight Cities (1947)

United States Strategic Bombing Survey, Effects of Air Attacks on Urban Complex Tokyo-Kawasaki-Yokohama (1947)*

United States Strategic Bombing Survey, Japanese Air Power (1946)*

United States Strategic Bombing Survey, Japanese Air Weapons and Tactics (1947)*

Wolf, William, *Boeing B-29 Superfortress – The Ultimate Look: From Drawing Board to VJ-Day* (Schiffer Military History, 2005)

* available online

INDEX

Figures in **bold** refer to illustrations.

air defense 8, **14**, **37**, 48–49, 61, 69
air power 9, 35–36, 38, **59**
antiaircraft artillery 6, 53, 55, 74
antiaircraft guns 6, 54, 67
assembly lines 8, **16**, 17, 24, 36
Atsugi airfield **28**, **37**, 49, 68, 70, **76**, 77

Boeing 7, 9, **10**, 11, **13**, **14**, 21, **22**, 36
   B-17 Flying Fortress 7–8, 10–11, 17, 21, 28, 41, 43, **44**, 49, 59
   B-17E 8, 19, **20**
   B-17F 44
   B-29 Superfortress **4**, 5–9, **11**, **12**, **13**, **14**, **19**, 21, **22**, **23**, **24**, **25**, **26**, 27, **28**, 29–32, 34, **36**, **38**, **39**, 40–41, **42**, **43**, **44**, 45, **47**, **48**, **50**, 51, 52, **53**, **54**, 55, **56**, **57**, **59**, **60**, 61, **62**, 63, **66**, 67–69, **70**, **71**, **72**, 73, **74**, 75, **76**, **77**, 78
   Model 299: 10
   Model 316: 10
   Model 333: 7
   Model 334: 11
   Model 335: 7, 11
   XB-15: 10, 11
   XB-19: 11, 23
   XB-29: 11, 13
   XB-30: 11, 13
   XB-31: 11, 13
   XB-32: 11
Bombardment Squadron (BS)
   24th BS/8th **66**
   324th BS/91st 44
   393rd BS/509th 8
   395th BS/40th **14**
   870th BS/497th **13**
bomb-bays 10, 22, 52, **53**, 57, **60**, 63
Bombardment Wing
   58th BW 68–69
   73rd BW 44, **55**
   313th BW **4**, 8
   314th BW **50**
   315th BW 53
bombers **4**, 5–10, **11**, **13**, 14, 19, 21, **22**, 23–24, 25, **26**, 27, 29–30, 33, 35–36, 39–42, **48**, 50–51, 53, **55**, 56, 57, 59–63, **66**, 67–70, **71**, 72–75, **76**
   dive-bomber **48**
   escorts 16–17
   four-engined **10**, 11, 28, 36, 41, **61**
   heavy 9–10, 17, 19, 35–36, **42**, 44, 61
   interceptors 17, 31
   long-range 7, 9, 16, 36
   strategic 9–10, 35–36
   stream 57, 59, 61, 68
   super 7, 11, 23, 36
   torpedo 16, **48**
   twin-engined **10**, 15
bombload 9, **13**, **37**, 51, 62

cannon
   20mm 7, 11, 15, 17, **19**, 20, 24, 31, 33, **63**, 72, 75
   downward-firing 20, **60**
   forward-firing 16, **34**
   Ho-3: 16
   Ho-5 20mm **19**, **27**, 30–32, **68**
   Ho-203 37mm 19, **30**, 58
   obliquely firing 19–20, 72, 75
   Type 99 20mm 7, 17, 19, **20**, 29–33, **66**
   upward-firing **60**
cockpit 14, 17, **20**, 28, 50, **52**, 56, **58**, 72
Consolidated **10**, **11**
   B-24 Liberator 11, 21, 28, 41–42, 44, 49, 59
   B-24D 8, **20**
   B-32 Dominator **11**, 13, 36

Endo, Lt(jg) Sachio **70**
engines 14–15, 17, 22–24, 28, **29**, 58, **66**

General Electric 13, 24–25
Ground Control Interception (GCI) 55, 62, 74
Guam 8, **50**

Hiroshima 8, 70, 76
Home Islands 5, 8, **36**, **38**, 39, 47–49, **61**, **68**, 69, 74, 76
Honshu 4, **37**, **48**, 68–69

Imperial Iron and Steel Works 8, 53, 68–69
Imperial Japanese Army (IJA) 4–5, 38, 46
Imperial Japanese Army Air Force (IJAAF)
   4th Hiko Sentai **48**, 68–69
   53rd Hiko Sentai **19**, **47**, **57**, **68**
   210th Kokutai **48**
   251st Kokutai 7, **16**, **19**, **20**, 49, **72**
   302nd Kokutai **20**, **28**, 49, 68, **70**, **76**, 77
   332nd Kokutai 69
   352nd Kokutai 69, **70**
Imperial Japanese Naval Air Force (IJNAF) **4**, 5–8, **16**, 17, 19–20, 28–29, 31–34, **36**, **37**, 40, 45, **46**, 47–49, 55–56, 60–61, **66**, 68–71, 74–77
Imperial Japanese Navy (IJN) 4, **5**, 16, 19, 38, 45–46, 49
incendiaries **6**, 8, 24, 30–31, 36, 51, 54, **55**, 62, 75
   M-47: **53**
   M-69: **53**, 54
   raids 8, **13**, **39**, 44, **54**, **56**, 72, 77
intelligence 4, 41, 55
interceptor 14, 17, 19, 31, 55–57, **62**, **63**, **66**, 74–75
Isley Field 8, **13**
Iwo Jima 8, **74**

Kawasaki 5, 7–8, 15–16, 28, **61**, 69
Kobe 8, **37**, **56**, 70–72
Kozono, Lt Cdr Yasuna 7, 19, **49**, 77
Kuramoto, SFPO Juzo 71, **72**, 75
Kure **37**, 68–70
Kurotori, Ens Shiro 71, **72**
landing gear 10, 21, 28, **52**
LeMay, Maj Gen Curtis 6, 8, **38**, 39, 45, **50**, 61–63, 66, 71–72, 74
Luftwaffe 14–15, 17, 36

machine guns 15, 30, 51, **63**
   0.50-cal. 11, **13**, 15, 24, 43, 63, 75
   7.7mm 16–17, 28
   7.92mm 30
   12.7mm 8, 17, 30, 31
   AN/M2 Browning 24–25, 30–31
Marianas **4**, 5, 8, **36**, **37**, 38–9, 45, 69–71, 73, 78
Matsudo **19**, **47**, **57**, **68**
Mitsubishi 7, 15–17
   A5M 16
   G3M 16
   G4M Rikko 72
   Ha-102: 28
   JM2 Raiden 68
   Ki-46 "Dinah" **27**
monoplanes **10**, 15, **27**
Morgan, Robert K. **44**

Nagasaki 8, **37**, 69
Nagoya 8, **37**, **48**, **61**, 68, 70
Nakajima 7, 15, **16**, 17, 19, 28, **29**
nightfighters 4, 14, **15**, **16**, **19**, **20**, 25, 27, **28**, **30**, 31–34, 40–41, 45, **48**, 49–53, 55, **59**, **60**, 61, **62**, 63, **66**, 68–69, **70**, **71**, 72–73, **74**, 75, **76**, 77–78
   D4Y2-S Suisei 76
   Gekko (Moonlight) nightfighter 19, **20**, 30–31, **34**, 59, **62**, **66**, **70**, 72, 75, **76**, **78**
   J1N1: 7–8, **16**, 17, 25, 27–28, **29**, 33, **34**, 49, **59**,

69–70, 77, **78**
J1N1-C 7, **16**, **19**, 31, 32, 49, 78
J1N1-S 31, 33, **48**, 76
Ki-45: 7–8, **15**, 16, 25–29, 31–32, 69–70, **71**, 78
Ki-45 KAI 7, 19, 48
Ki-45 KAIa 8, 27
Ki-45 KAIc 8, 18, 19, 27, 29, 30, 31–33, 47, 57, 58, 59, 60, 61, 68, **76**, 78
night raids 5, 14, 25, 45, 51–55, 61–63, 68–69, 71–73
North Field 4, 8

Omura 69–70
Operation *Hailstone* 45
Operation *Matterhorn* 39, **43**
Operation *Starvation* 8, 39
ordnance 8, 10, 27, 62, 69
Osaka 8, 33, **37**, 44, 68, 70–72, 76

radar **5**, 6, 15, 20, 50, 53, 66, 69, **72**, 74–75
   air intercept (AI) **20**, 25, **28**, 32–33, **34**, 56, **66**, 74–75, **76**
   AN/ARN-7: **26**
   AN/APQ-4: 26
   AN/APQ-7: 26, 53
   AN/APQ-9: 26
   AN/APQ-13: 26
   AN/APS-15: 26
   AN/APR-4: 26
   early-warning 4, **5**, 55, 57
   FD-2: **20**, **28**, 33, **34**, 75, **76**
   ground-based 56, 66–67
   jamming 26–27, 53, **55**
   SCR-720: 75
   station 4–5, **36**, **37**
   TAMA3: 33–34
   Type 3, Mark 1, Model 3: **5**
Request For Proposals (RFP) 7, 10, 23
Royal Air Force (RAF) 9, 15, 35–36

Saipan 8, **13**, 26, 44, 69
Sasebo **37**, 69
searchlights **20**, 56, 63, 69
Shimonoseki 8, **37**, 68

tail gunner 22, 24, 59, **63**, 66
Tinian 4, 8, **66**, **77**
Tokyo **4**, **5**, **6**, 8, **13**, **19**, 26, **37**, 39, 44, **47**, 49, **50**, 51, 53, **54**, **55**, **57**, **66**, 68, 70–71, **72**, **75**, 76–77
turrets 13, **22**, **24**, 25, 43, 51–52, 59, 63
   forward **13**, 24
   gun 21, **22**, 25
   lower 24–25, 66
   power **24**, 25, 43
   remotely controlled 25, 36
   tail **24**, 45, 66

US Army 9, 24, 36
US Army Air Corps (USAAC) 7, 9, **10**, **11**, 13, 23, 36, 41–42, 44
US Army Air Force (USAAF)
   Twentieth Air Force 6, **67**, 73, **74**, 75, **77**, 78
      XX Bomber Command **38**, 39, 41, 61, 69–70, 73, 75
      XXI Bomber Command 6, 8, 39–41, 45, **50**, 51, **55**, 67, 70–71, 73, 76–77

Wichita **13**, **14**, 42

Yawata 8, 53, 68–70, 75
Yokohama 5, **55**
Yokosuka 19, **28**, **37**, 68
   Air Arsenal 19, 49
   Kokutai **20**, 71, **72**
   Naval Station **37**, **72**, **76**